Module E (Scots) – Contents

The suggested answers presented in this booklet are longer and generally more detailed than those expected from a candidate taking the examinations. These answers are intended to provide candidates with an indicative guide to the form and standard of answer which they should try to provide. The suggested answer may not contain all the points that could correctly be made and candidates should note that credit will be awarded for valid answers which may not be fully covered in this booklet.

Typeset by Pindar plc, Scarborough, North Yorkshire.

Printed by Bell and Bain Ltd, Glasgow

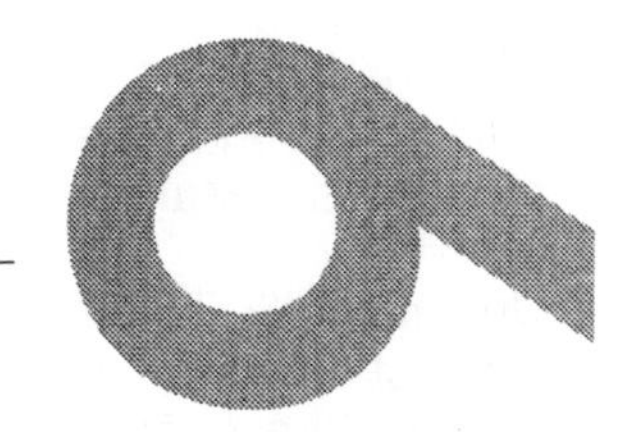

Module E – Professional Stage

Information for Control and Decision Making

December 1996

Question Paper:	
Time allowed	**3 hours**
This paper is divided into two sections	
Section A	TWO questions ONLY to be answered
Section B	TWO questions ONLY to be answered

Section A – TWO questions ONLY to be attempted

1 Tritex plc produces a number of products which pass through three consecutive processes – Making, Converting and Finishing – before sale to customers.

Until recently, Tritex plc has prepared standard product costs per unit for each product using (a) control standards and (b) current standards. Appendix 1 shows extracts from these standards for Product A. These standards plus a detailed variance analysis have been the main focus of control information. The control standards are based on industry average performance and the current standards are based on the level of performance which it is anticipated should be attainable using last year's actual performance as the starting point.

The control and current standard product costs per unit incorporate the following specifications:

- Process losses (%) are expressed as a percentage of input to each process.
- Material requirement is based on the input to the Making process.
- Labour requirement is based on the total hours per unit of output from a process.
- Variable overhead is absorbed on the basis of net processing hours (i.e. excluding idle time) per unit of output from a process.
- Variable overhead is absorbed into all products using an average rate per net processing hour.
- Work-in-progress is 100% complete at the end of each process.

Tritex plc has produced amended unit standard process costs which incorporate Activity Based Costing (ABC) and the planned effects of a Total Quality Management (TQM) programme. Appendix 1 shows an extract of such a standard cost for product A.

The ABC/TQM standard costs incorporate the following in their specification:

- Zero idle time allowance for labour. Employees will carry out some rework material handling and maintenance not previously included in the standard labour cost.
- The cost driver for all variable overhead in the Making process is the number of steam operations per product unit and overhead is absorbed on this basis. For product A this should result in an overhead cost reduction of 30 % per product unit from the control standard cost. Any residual difference is due to improved work practices.

Required:

(a) **Prepare workings which show the calculation of the appropriate values in the cells marked (?) in the Current Standard Cost for product A in Appendix 1, (See page 4).**

(6 marks)

(b) **As a benchmarking exercise, discuss the differences between the control standard and current standards for product A (per Appendix 1), highlighting possible reasons for such differences.**

(9 marks)

(c) **Use the ABC/TQM standard for product A together with information provided in the question to indicate specific ways in which Tritex plc is proposing to implement a total quality philosophy. Your answer should include discursive and quantitative elements.**

(12 marks)

(d) Standard costing and variance analysis provides some control information. Adoption of a total quality philosophy will require additional information from the control system.
Identify and comment on the additional information which may be provided where a total quality philosophy is adopted.

(8 marks)

(35 marks)

Appendix to Question 1

Extracts from standard product cost per unit – Product A for each of Current Standard, Control Standard, ABC/TQM Standard

	Losses	Product Units	sqm/unit hours/unit steam ops./unit (see note 1)	rate/sqm rate/hour rate/ steam op.	Cost	WIP value per unit
	%			£	£	£
Current Standard Cost						
Making Process (input)	9·0%	?				
Raw material			6·720	0·85	?	
Labour			0·142	4·75	?	
Overheads			0·125	7·00	?	
sub-total making					?	?
Converting Process (input)	13·0%	?				
Finishing Process (input)	7·0%	?				
Control Standard Cost						
Making Process (input)	5·0%	1·2312				
Raw material			6·000	0·80	5·910	
Labour			0·108	5·00	0·632	
Overheads			0·100	6·32	0·739	
sub-total making					7·281	6·225
Converting Process (input)	10·0%	1·1696				
Finishing Process (input)	5·0%	1·0526				
ABC/TQM Standard Cost						
Making Process (input)	1·0%	1·0465				
Raw material			6·000	0·90	5·651	
Labour			0·095	6·00	0·591	
Overheads			1·000	0·36	0·373	
sub-total making					6·615	6·385
Converting Process (input)	2·5%	1·0360				
Finishing Process (input)	1·0%	1·0101				

Note 1: The charge basis per unit for material, labour and overhead (and corresponding cost per unit) will be one of the above. The specific basis (and cost) which will apply for a particular expense type may vary for each of current, control and ABC/TQM standards. The information provided in the question gives the details from which you can determine the relevant basis in each case.

2 A holiday resort operates a clifftop cable car to transport tourists to and from the beach during the holiday season.

During the 1996 season the following operating information applied:

(i) Average variable cost per single cable car journey was £10.

(ii) Total fixed cost for the season was £48,000.

(iii) The fare structure incorporates a return fare which gives a 10% saving as compared to paying for two single journeys. The fares per single journey were as follows: Adult £1·00; Juvenile £0·60; Senior Citizen £0·50.

(iv) The cable car has a maximum capacity of 30 passengers per journey. It operated for 100 journeys per day on each of 120 days during 1996.

(v) Total passenger journeys represented 60% capacity utilisation per journey. The capacity utilised comprised 50% adult, 30% juvenile and 20% senior citizen journeys. For all passenger categories, 75% of the tickets sold were for single journey fares and the remainder for return fares.

(vi) Advertising revenue from displays in the cable car totalled £20,000. This is a fixed annual sum from contracts which will apply each season up to and including 1998.

It is anticipated that costs will increase by 5% due to inflation during the 1997 season and that fares will also increase by 5% from the 1996 levels. While the fare increase has been agreed and cannot be altered, it is possible that the inflation effect on costs may differ from the forecast rate of 5%.

Required:

(a) Prepare a statement showing the budgeted net profit or loss for the 1997 season where capacity utilisation per journey and passenger mix is expected to be the same as in 1996, but the number of cable car journeys per day will be increased to 120 journeys, with the same length of operating season.
(All relevant workings must be shown). (7 marks)

(b) Explain the meaning of the information in the two-way datatable shown in Appendix 2 which has been extracted from a spreadsheet model of the situation and comment on the range of values including reference to your answer to part (a). (6 marks)

(c) Capacity utilisation and the rate of inflation have been identified as key variables for 1997. Probabilities have been estimated for the level at which the key variables will occur. Capacity utilisation and inflation are independent of each other. The estimates are as follows:

Capacity Utilisation %	*Probability*	*Inflation %*	*Probability*
80	0·15	2	0·2
60	0·60	5	0·5
40	0·25	8	0·3

(i) **Prepare a summary which shows the range of possible net profit or loss outcomes, showing the combined probability of each outcome, using Appendix 2 as appropriate.**

(8 marks)

(ii) **Calculate the expected value of net profit or loss, indicating how you arrived at your answer.** (2 marks)

(iii) **Using your answer to c(i), calculate the cumulative probability of the net profit being greater than £30,000.**

(2 marks)

(d) **Calculate the percentage of maximum capacity at which the cable car will breakeven during 1997 where the variables are as used in the calculations in (a), except that an amended inflation rate has resulted in total costs of £205,440.**

(6 marks)

(e) **Explain ways in which a spreadsheet model could be used to calculate the effect of EACH of the following variable data changes on profit for 1997 where all other variables remain unchanged:**
(i) Changes in passenger mix
(ii) Changes in the overall fare increase between 1% and 10% in steps of 1%. *(No calculations required).*

(4 marks)

(35 marks)

Appendix 2

Two-way datatable monitoring changes in net profit for a range of levels of capacity utilisation and inflation.

		Capacity utilisation (%)				
		20%	*40%*	*60%*	*80%*	*100%*
	1%	–104927	–35935	33058	102050	17104
	2%	–106847	–37855	31138	100130	16912
	3%	–108767	–39775	29218	98210	16720
	4%	–110687	–41695	27298	96290	16528
	5%	–112607	–43615	25378	94370	16336
Inflation (%)	*6%*	–114527	–45535	23458	92450	16144
	7%	–116447	–47455	21538	90530	15952
	8%	–118367	–49375	19618	88610	15760
	9%	–120287	–51295	17698	86690	15568
	10%	–122207	–53215	15778	84770	15376

3 The budget for the Production, Planning and Development Department of Obba plc. is currently prepared as part of a traditional budgetary planning and control system. The analysis of costs by expense type for the period ended 30 November 1996 where this system is in use is as follows:

Expense type	Budget	Actual
	%	%
Salaries	60	63
Supplies	6	5
Travel cost	12	12
Technology cost	10	7
Occupancy cost	12	13

The total budget and actual costs for the department for the period ended 30 November 1996 are £1,000,000 and £1,060,000 respectively.

The company now feels that an Activity Based Budgeting approach should be used. A number of activities have been identified for the Production, Planning and Development Department. An investigation has indicated that total budget and actual costs should be attributed to the activities on the following basis:

	Budget	*Actual*
Activities:	*%*	*%*
1. Routing/scheduling – new products	20	16
2. Routing/scheduling – existing products	40	34
3. Remedial re-routing/scheduling	5	12
4. Special studies – specific orders	10	8
5. Training	10	15
6. Management & administration	15	15

Required:

(a) (i) **Prepare TWO budget control statements for the Production Planning and Development Department for the period ended 30 November 1996 which compare budget with actual cost and show variances using**
1. a traditional expense based analysis and
2. an activity based analysis. (6 marks)

(ii) **Identify and comment on FOUR advantages claimed for the use of Activity Based Budgeting over traditional budgeting using the Production Planning and Development example to illustrate your answer.**
(12 marks)

(iii) **Comment on the use of the information provided in the activity based statement which you prepared in (i) in activity based performance measurement and suggest additional information which would assist in such performance measurement.**
(8 marks)

[P.T.O.

(b) Other activities have been identified and the budget quantified for the three months ended 31 March 1997 as follows:

Activities	*Cost Driver Unit basis*	*Units of Cost Driver*	*Cost*
			£000
Product design	design hours	8,000	2,000 (*see note 1)*
Purchasing	purchase orders	4,000	200
Production	machine hours	12,000	1,500 (*see note 2)*
Packing	volume (cu.m.)	20,000	400
Distribution	weight (kg)	120,000	600

Note 1: this includes all design costs for new products released this period.
Note 2: this includes a depreciation provision of £300,000 of which £8,000 applies to 3 months depreciation on a straight line basis for a new product (NPD). The remainder applies to other products.

New product NPD is included in the above budget. The following additional information applies to NPD:
(i) Estimated total output over the product life cycle: 5,000 units (4 years life cycle).
(ii) Product design requirement: 400 design hours
(iii) Output in quarter ended 31 March 1997: 250 units
(iv) Equivalent batch size per purchase order: 50 units
(v) Other product unit data: production time 0·75 machine hours; volume 0·4 cu.metres; weight 3 kg.

Required:

Prepare a unit overhead cost for product NPD using an activity based approach which includes an appropriate share of life cycle costs using the information provided in (b) above.

(9 marks)

(35 marks)

Section B – TWO questions ONLY to be attempted

4 Performance in education or training institutions may be viewed in the context of the performance of the institution and the performance of staff.

(a) Briefly discuss each of FIVE performance measures, including financial and non-financial measures, which may be used.

(10 marks)

(b) Discuss the motivational factors likely to influence the level of performance of staff and suggest ways in which efforts may be made to quantify such factors.

(5 marks)

(15 marks)

5 Strategic decisions may involve dealing with steady, increased or decreased demand for any particular product or its discontinuance.

(a) "Alternative valuation bases and relevant costs may be used for the valuation of units of a product". Discuss this statement in the context of decision making for:
(i) disposal of existing product units no longer required
(ii) replacement of product units to meet current demand
(iii) increase in the level of product units as demand increases
(iv) decrease in the level of product units as demand falls

(10 marks)

(b) Discuss how the timescale of the decision may affect the treatment of each of committed costs and discretionary costs in decision making.

(5 marks)

(15 marks)

6 **(a)** Spiro Division is part of a vertically integrated group of divisions all located in one country. All divisions sell externally and also transfer goods to other divisions within the group. Spiro Division performance is measured using profit before tax as a performance measure.

(i) **Prepare an outline statement which shows the costs and revenue elements which should be included in the calculation of divisional profit before tax.**

(4 marks)

(ii) **The degree of autonomy which is allowed to divisions may affect the absolute value of profit reported.**
Discuss this statement in relation to Spiro Division.

(6 marks)

(b) Discuss the pricing basis on which divisions should offer to transfer goods in order that corporate profit maximising decisions should take place.

(5 marks)

(15 marks)

End of Question Paper

Answers

1 (a) Input to Finishing = 1/0·93 = 1·0753
Input to Converting = 1·0753/0·87 = 1·2360
Input to Making = 1·2360/0·91 = 1·3582

Raw material cost (based on input)		
= 1·3582 × 6·72 × 0·85	=	£7·758
Labour cost (based on output)		
= 1·236 × 0·142 × 4·75	=	0·834
Overhead cost (based on output)		
= 1·236 × 0·125 × 7·00	=	1·082
Sub-total Making	=	£9·674

Work-in-progress per unit = £9·674/1·236 = £7·827

(b) A number of differences may be noted when comparing the control standard and current standard costs for product A:

– Process losses(%) are considerably higher in the current standard. This may be due to factors such as lack of training of employees, poor machine performance, lack of motivation, sacrifice of quality for speed of throughput.
– The current standard specification includes 12% more material (sqm.) which has a price per sqm. which is 5p above the control standard. The extra material may be due to product specification differences which may indicate the need for a design review by Tritex. The price difference could indicate better quality material but could also indicate a less efficient purchasing function.
– Net labour hours per unit (0·125 to 0·100 hours) are 25% greater in the current standard. In addition, idle time is greater. For the current standard idle time is 12% of input labour as compared with 8% in the control standard. Labour rate of pay per hour in the current standard is 25p lower than in the control standard. The greater operating time and higher idle time may be due in part to a less skilled grade of labour being used. Operating time may be higher because of lack of training, poor motivation, poor machine performance. Idle time may be higher because of expected levels of machine breakdown and poor production flow (e.g. waiting for raw materials).
– Overheads are incurred at a higher rate per hour in the current standard (£7 to £6·32). This may be due to the efficiency with which overhead items are sourced externally or provided internally (e.g. maintenance), and/or due to the price at which they are obtained. In addition, the overheads are absorbed on the basis of processing time which is higher per unit in the current standard. It may be that processing time is not the relevant cost driver for such overheads.

(c) Total quality management embraces continuous improvement aiming at features such as zero defects at minimum cost, supply of quality products at the agreed design specification on a right-first-time basis, elimination of waste, elimination of non-value added activities.

The ABC/TQM standard cost for product A shows:
– A low level of process losses. This indicates a move towards the zero defects aim of TQM.
– Raw material input is 6sqm. per unit which is the same as the control standard. The price per sqm. is £0·90 which is higher than the control standard (£0·80). This may indicate a better quality material in order to provide the design specification required by customers. It may also indicate the cost of a just-in-time purchasing agreement which supplies materials of an agreed specification when required, thus reducing, for example, stock holding costs and returns of defective products from customers.

- The overall labour time per unit has fallen by approximately 12% from the control standard (0·108 to 0·095 hours)
  Labour cost now has zero idle time allowance and employees are expected to carry out some re-work, material handling and maintenance tasks. This indicates a TQM policy of having a highly skilled, well motivated, multi-task workforce who will embrace the zero defect, right-first-time philosophy. It will also help to reduce waste and non-value added activities.
  This labour environment seems to be achieved by paying premium rates of pay (£6 per hour) for highly skilled, well motivated employees.
- Overhead costs are being absorbed on the basis of steam operations per product unit which has been recognised as the cost driver rather than an average rate per operating hour. This appears to indicate that product A was being overcharged with overhead cost under the old system. The comparative rates per unit of product are:

Control standard = 0·1 × £6·32	=	£0·632
ABC/TQM standard = 1 × 0·36	=	0·360
Total saving	=	£0·272

  We are told that the reduction due to the recognition of the change in cost driver to steam operations per unit is 30% × £0·632 = £0·190. The residual saving of £0·082 (£0·272 – 0·90) is due to improved work practices as part of the TQM programme.

(d) The standard cost and variance analysis control system provides some information such as relative levels of process losses (yield variances) and efficiency and expenditure variances. There are, however, a number of additional features which a TQM environment linked to the use of non-financial indicators will require:

- TQM aims at continuous improvement. The focus should be on performance measures which illustrate a continuous trend rather than a 'steady state' standard performance which is accepted for a specific period.
- Many measures are not highlighted by the standard cost/variance system. Additional quantitative measures may be kept to monitor:
  - customer dissatisfaction (e.g. level of replacements of faulty goods, number of late deliveries)
  - high levels of stock losses (raw material, WIP, finished goods)
  - market share (is this growing, shrinking, changing?)
  - levels of non-value added activities (e.g. re-work, material handling)
- Increased focus may be placed on attempts to measure and value internal and external failure cost, appraisal costs and prevention costs in the operation of a TQM programme.
  (Marks will be awarded for alternative relevant comments in parts (b) to (d)).

2 (a) *Workings:*

Passenger journeys for 1997:

Maximum	120 × 120 × 30	=	432,000	
Planned	120 × 120 × 30 × 60%	=	259,200	
Single fare	259,200 × 75%	=	194,400	
Return fare	259,200 × 25%	=	64,800	(single journeys)

Inflation adjusted fares for 1997 per single journey equivalent:

	Single (£)	Return (£)
Adult	1·05	0·945
Juvenile	0·63	0·567
Senior Citizen	0·525	0·4725

Note: single fares are 1996 fares increased by 5%.
return fare equivalent includes 10% reduction
e.g. £1·05 × 90% = £0·945.

Budgeted Profit and Loss Statement 1997

			£	£
Revenue from fares				
Single	: Adult	194,400 × 50% × £1·05	102,060	
	: Juvenile	194,400 × 30% × £0·63	36,742	
	: Senior Citizen	194,400 × 20% × £0·525	20,412	
Return	: Adult	64,800 × 50% × £0·945	30,618	
	: Juvenile	64,800 × 30% × £0·567	11,022	
	: Senior Citizen	64,800 × 20% × £0·4725	6,124	206,978
Advertising revenue				20,000
Total Income				226,978
Less:				
Variable cost		120 × 120 × £10 × 1·05	151,200	
Fixed cost		£48,000 × 1·05	50,400	201,600
Net profit or loss				25,378

(All figures to nearest £)

(b) The two-way data table shows the net profit or loss for each of a range of combinations of capacity utilisation and inflation levels, using the variable data in a spreadsheet model of the situation.

The existing situation is for 60% capacity utilisation and an inflation effect of 5% on costs. Note that this gives a net profit of £25,378 as calculated in part (a) above.

The data table shows the best possible outcome as a profit of £171,043 at 100% capacity at 1% inflation. The worst possible outcome is a loss of £122,207 at 20% capacity and 10% inflation.

The data table indicates that breakeven point is between 40% and 60% capacity utilisation. The figures indicate that breakeven is likely to be at approximately 50% capacity utilisation at low inflation, moving towards 60% capacity utilisation at high levels of inflation.

(c) **(i)** The range of possible outcomes using the probability estimates quoted and values from Appendix 2 are:

Capacity Utilisation %	*Prob.*	*Inflation* %	*Prob.*	*Combined Prob.*	*Net profit /loss* £
80	0·15	2	0·2	0·03	100,130
		5	0·5	0·075	94,370
		8	0·3	0·045	88,610
60	0·6	2	0·2	0·12	31,138
		5	0·5	0·30	25,378
		8	0·3	0·18	19,618
40	0·25	2	0·2	0·05	–37,855
		5	0·5	0·125	–43,615
		8	0·3	0·075	–49,375
				1·000	

(ii) For each row in the above table, multiply the combined probability by the net profit or loss and sum the answers.
The expected value of net profit is £17,902·55.

(iii) The combined probability of a net profit of more than £30,000 is 0·03 + 0·075 + 0·045 + 0·12 = 0·27.

(d) For breakeven point total revenue = total cost
Total cost remains fixed for the number of journeys as does advertising revenue.

Total fares revenue changes as capacity utilisation changes.
At breakeven point we require total fares revenue = total cost minus advertising revenue = £205,440 – £20,000 = £185,440.

From part (a), revenue from fares at 60% capacity = £206,978
For breakeven, capacity utilisation = 185,440/206,978 = 89·6% of the budgeted level of 60% i.e. 89·6% × 60% = 53·8% of maximum capacity.

OR. an alternative approach is as follows:

let N = number of passenger journeys at breakeven
Hence 0·75N = single journeys and 0·25N = return journeys.
Using the mix of adult/juvenile/senior citizen journeys of 50%/30%/20%, the total number of journeys may be expressed as:

	Single	Return
Adult	0·375N	0·125N
Juvenile	0·225N	0·075N
Senior Citizen	0·15N	0·05N

e.g. adult single = 0·75N × 0·5 = 0·375N

Using the 1997 fares as calculated in (a) we can express total revenue in terms of N and equate this to total cost less advertising revenue for breakeven point.
0·375N × 1·05 + 0·225N × 0·63 + 0·15N x 0·525 + 0·125N × 0·945
+ 0·075N × 0·567 + 0·05N × 0·4725 = 205,440 – 20,000
Solving gives N = 232,228 journeys
maximum journeys = 432,000 (as calculated in (a))
Hence percentage capacity utilisation at breakeven
= 232,228/432,000 = 53·8%

(e) The spreadsheet may be used as a 'what-if' analysis tool by changing the values of any one or more variables on a one-off basis and noting the effect on profit or loss.

The passenger mix could be changed to (say) adult/juvenile/senior citizen of 40%/40%/20% and the amended net profit noted where all other variables remain unchanged. A similar procedure could be applied by changing the fare prices by (say) 3% and noting the amended profit.

The use of data tables will enable a range of changes in one or more variables to be monitored and summarised. A one-way data table could be prepared which would show the net profit or loss for fare increases of 1% to 10% in 1% steps.

3 (a) (i)

Production Planning and Development
Operating Statement for period ended 30 November 1996
(Traditional Expense based Analysis)

Expense	*Budget* *£000*	*Actual* *£000*	*Variance* *£000*
Salaries	600	667·8	67·8(A)
Supplies	60	53·0	7·0(F)
Travel cost	120	127·2	7·2(A)
Technology cost	100	74·2	25·8(F)
Occupancy cost	120	137·8	17·8(A)
Total	1,000	1,060·0	60·0(A)

Production Planning and Development
Operating Statement for period ended 30 November 1996
(Activity based Analysis)

Activity	*Budget* *£000*	*Actual* *£000*	*Variance* *£000*
Routing/scheduling – new products	200	169·6	30·4(F)
Routing/scheduling – existing products	400	360·4	39·6(F)
Remedial re-routing/scheduling	50	127·2	77·2(A)
Special studies – specific orders	100	84·8	15·2(F)
Training	100	159·0	59·0(A)
Management and Administration	150	159·0	9·0(A)
Total	1,000	1,060·0	60·0(A)

Note: (A) = adverse (F) = favourable

(ii) Advantages claimed for the use of activity based budgeting include:

1. Resource allocation is linked to a strategic plan for the future, prepared after considering alternative strategies.
   Traditional budgets tend to focus on resources and inputs rather than on objectives and alternatives. In the question, the traditional budget focuses on overall expenditure on resources such as salaries and the overall expenditure variance.
2. New high priority activities are encouraged rather than focusing on the existing planning model.
   Activity based budgeting focuses on activities. This allows the identification of the cost of each activity e.g. Special studies. It facilitates focus on control of the resources required to provide the activity. It will also help where financial constraints exist in that activities may be ranked and their importance considered, rather than arbitrary cuts being made in areas such as production planning and development.
3. There is more focus on efficiency and effectiveness and the alternative methods by which they may be achieved.
   Activity based budgeting assists in the operation of a total quality philosophy. Focus within individual activities can be on areas such as waste reduction, inefficiency removal, innovation in methods.
4. It avoids arbitrary cuts in specific budget areas in order to meet overall financial targets.
   Activities 1, 2 and 4 in the budget in (i) are primary activities which add value to products. Activity 3 (remedial re-scheduling) is a non-value added activity which should be eliminated. Activities 5 and 6 (Training and Management) are secondary activities which support the primary activities. Efforts should be made to ensure that their objectives are achieved in an efficient manner at minimum cost.

5. It tends to lead to increased management commitment to the budget process.
   This should be achieved since the activity analysis enables management to focus on the objectives of each activity. Identification of primary, secondary and non-value added activities should also help in motivating management in activity planning and control.

(iii) In assessing the performance of an activity we must measure its cost and the quality of its provision.

The statement in (i) shows the budget v actual cost comparison for each activity. This indicates that cost has fallen in all three primary activities – development of routing, existing routing and special studies. Remedial re-routing is double the budget level which must be investigated since it is a non-value added activity. Training cost has increased by 50% from budget. This may be related to the high level of remedial re-routing where staff under training have not been performing efficiently.

For each activity it is also possible to prepare a cost analysis which compares budget v actual resources for salaries, etc in a similar way to the overall traditional budget statement given in the question. This will enable investigation of factors such as why salary costs for the activity exceed budget by £X'000 or why supplies are below budget by £Y'000.

The cost information does not specify the cost driver for each activity and the budget v actual comparison of these. For example staff hours is likely to be the cost driver for an activity such as routing/scheduling whereas for training the cost driver may be number of staff trained. It is also necessary to determine the efficient cost driver level e.g. staff hours per individual route development for a new product. How does this compare with the actual staff hours per individual route development? Again, a comparison of budget cost versus actual cost per staff member trained will give an indication of efficiency of provision of the activity.

A further aspect of performance measurement is to determine the "root cause" of each cost driver. For example the staff hours required per route designed may be linked to the level of technology and software systems used. The root cause of employee training may be high labour turnover due to poor career prospects or a stressful work environment. It is important that such root causes are identified, since continuous improvement of the provision of an activity will only be achieved through improvement in the factors which influence its incidence.

(b) Calculate the cost per unit of cost driver for each activity.
For example for purchasing, rate per purchase order = £200,000/4,000 = £50.
Additional workings are detailed as required for individual activities.

Activity based overhead cost per unit of product NPD

		£
Product design (note 1)	0·08 hours × £250	20
Purchasing (note 2)	0·02 orders × £50	1
Production (note 3)	0·75 machine hours × £100	75
Depreciation (note 4)		25·60
Packing	0·4 cu.metres × £20	8
Distribution	3kg x £5	15
Total		144·60

Note 1: design hours per unit over product life = 400/5,000 = 0·08 hours.
Note 2: purchase orders per unit = 1/50 = 0·02 orders.
Note 3: machine costs (excluding depreciation)
= £1,500,000 – £300,000 = £1,200,000
cost per machine hour = £1,200,000/12,000 = £100
Note 4: asset cost over life of product
= £8,000 × 4 quarters × 4 years = £128,000
depreciation per product unit = £128,000/5,000 = £25·60.

4 *The answer to this question could be framed in the context of one of a range of education or training institutions. The answer which follows is written with reference to a possible set of circumstances for a UK university. Answers framed in the context of another type of institution would be equally acceptable.*

(a) Performance measurement requires confirmation that the mission statement of the institution is being implemented on a continuing basis. Performance measures which may be used include financial performance, competitiveness, quality of service, flexibility, resource utilisation and innovation.

Financial performance: the key measure will be cost per graduate. This can be monitored through time to see if real savings are being achieved and also measured against competing institutions.

Competitive performance: this will be measured in terms of the student population attracted to the institution. The growth rate may be measured in total and by course. In addition, the 'hit rate' i.e. the ratio of uptake to applications may be monitored by course.

Quality of service: this is a contentious issue which will include the quality of academic input, academic environment and ancillary support services such as student accommodation, health and financial advice. Quality may be measured in terms of throughput rate i.e. percentage of students who obtain a qualification and the proportion of honours to ordinary graduates. It may also be measured through student responses to questionnaires on issues such as tutoring, handout material and advice from staff. Measurement of quality may also be attempted through staff review programmes and internal reviews of the effectiveness of committee structures in the institution.

Flexibility: this may be measured in terms of modes of learning environment on offer including full-time, part-time and distance learning study. A further measure of flexibility is the availability of intermediate entry and exit points to courses in order to allow for variations in qualifications held by students on entry and to ensure that an intermediate exit qualification is available for students who do not perform to their expectations or who leave for financial or personal reasons.

Resource utilisation: the main resources are staff and accommodation. A key performance measure is the student:staff ratio. This may be measured for each course, department or faculty and monitored against targets and through time. The percentage fill of accommodation is another useful resource measure.

Innovation: examples may include the type of course provided, such as moves into new and topical course areas such as a degree in environmental accounting. Innovation may also be measured by the type of learning environment. For example, a multi-mode approach may be offered where students can study partly by distance learning and partly by attendance at classes. Innovation in teaching and learning methods may include the use of interactive multi-media material.

(Other relevant points would be accepted.)

(b) Agency theory sees the employee as the agent for a task where the outcome will depend on the effort put into the task by the employee. Expectancy theory states that the individual chooses his/her actions based on valence and expectancy. Valence may be intrinsic, such as a feeling of competence, or extrinsic such as the level of bonus, promotion, attendance at conferences. Expectancy is derived from the perceived probabilities that such rewards will follow from a given set of actions. This will apply to academic staff in the same way as in any other work environment.

Performance may also be affected by the attitudes of staff summarised in terms such as 'pride in work' or 'professional attitude'. Behaviouralists will also argue that positions on Maslow's hierarchy of human needs will influence the attitude of staff to work. Consider the higher level needs of belonging, esteem and self-actualisation. In the academic context, the lecturer may belong to a group of peers with similar academic goals; gain esteem from the achievement of goals such as the publication of research papers; gain self actualisation through being a main contributor in new course design or innovative teaching methods.

The measurement of performance may be viewed in a number of ways including:
(i) The number of papers published in research journals.
(ii) Pass rates in courses in which the staff member is involved.
(iii) Staff review procedures by peers or immediate superiors.
(iv) Results of responses to student questionnaires on various aspects of staff performance and attitude.

(Other relevant points would be accepted).

5 **(a)** **(i)** Disposal of existing product units which are no longer required means that the price at which the product could be sold in the past is no longer relevant. Historical costs are irrelevant in the circumstances. The important measure is the net realisable value of the units. The calculation of net realisable value will depend on the circumstances of disposal. It may be that the units can be sold for an alternative use after further work has been carried out on them. The relevant costs are those directly associated with the alteration for sale. It may be that the units can only be sold as scrap after incurring disposal costs such as transport or break-up costs. This could leave a negative net realisable value where additional costs exceed scrap revenue.

(ii) When units are being replaced to meet current demand, replacement cost is the relevant value for decision making purposes. This may be the same as the current valuation on a full cost basis including direct costs plus an absorbed share of indirect costs. It may be, however, that replacement costs will rise e.g. because of increases in the price of inputs or the need for the replacement of assets used in the production process. In this situation it may also be relevant to know the cost of external sourcing as the replacement basis, in order that a make or buy decision can be made.

(iii) A decision relating to the impact of an increase in output level should only include incremental or additional costs caused directly by the increase in output. Existing fixed costs which will now support the larger total output should be ignored. However, any new or 'incremental' fixed costs should be included. Variable costs may also fall where the increased activity level results in economies of scale such as better purchasing agreements with suppliers or lower machine costs through increased efficiency of operation at higher activity levels.

It may be that the expanded activity level will require the acquisition of additional resources e.g. additional machinery or factory space or the payment of a salary to additional supervisors. In this way the additional contribution, if any, to be obtained from the increased output may be calculated.

(iv) Where the level of activity is to fall, any decision should only take into account those costs which will change as a result of the decision. These are avoidable costs which must be distinguished from committed or sunk costs. As demand falls, some fixed costs may be avoidable e.g. salary of a supervisor no longer required, while others will remain e.g. occupancy costs of production space. There may be a negative aspect to avoidable costs in that some variable costs may increase because of the lower level of activity e.g. higher purchasing costs and machine operating costs.

(b) Committed costs are viewed as those which must be incurred irrespective of the decision taken. Timescale is important in such a classification. It is a well known view in Economics that 'in the very long run, all costs are variable while in the very short run all costs are fixed'. An example would be the leasing costs for a building. If a lease is renewable each year, this is quite different when cost classification is being made, from a lease to which the company is committed for 20 years. For a short-term decision relating to (say) a three year period, the long-term lease is a committed cost which should be excluded, whereas the short-term lease is incremental each year and should be included.

Discretionary costs are those in which management judgement is an important factor. The decision maker has discretion as to whether it is relevant and necessary to incur such costs. Examples may be as divergent as expenditure on research and development, staff training or operation of a management accounting function. For short-term decision making it may be argued that such costs are not directly relevant to a particular project e.g. should we undertake a one-off contract. For longer term decisons, however, the discretionary nature of such costs is reduced. In order to maintain market share and develop new materials, research and development expenditure is vital. Staff training is required to ensure continuing high quality input in the provision of goods and services to customers. The management accounting function is (we hope!) of value in assisting management in planning, control and decision making.

6 (a) (i) A summary of the calculation of divisional profit may be shown as:

	£
Sales to outside customers	XXXX
Inter-divisional sales	XXXX
	XXXX
Less:	
Variable costs of goods sold	(XXXX)
Variable divisional expenses	(XXXX)
Controllable contribution	XXXX
less: Controllable divisional fixed costs	(XXXX)
Controllable profit before tax	XXXX
less: Head Office costs	(XXXX)
Net profit before tax	XXXX

(ii) The degree of autonomy allowed to a division will affect the extent to which divisional management can control various aspects of income and expenditure. A number of illustrations of this are as follows:

- The ratio of internal transfers to other divisions to external sales may be determined to a greater extent by divisional management where an increased level of autonomy is given. Where internal transfers take place at a lower price than external sales, an increased proportion of transfers will result in a decreased profit reported at the division.
- The degree of autonomy will also affect the transfer price policy of each division. Where a fully directed central pricing policy is applied, the transfer price may be as low as marginal cost where spare capacity exists at the transferring division. This will reduce the profit reported at Spiro Division for goods which it is transferring out to other divisions. Conversely it will increase its reported profit for goods which are transferred in from other divisions for further processing before sale.
- Where complete autonomy is given to divisions, Spiro Division may increase its reported profit by purchasing a component from an outside source at a price which is lower than the lowest internal transfer price available. This will increase its absolute reported profit but may not be in the best interests of the group if spare capacity exists at one or more of the supplying divisions within the group.
- The level of costs incurred and hence profit reported at Spiro Division may be affected by the degree of autonomy allowed. It may be that some costs are reduced through local purchasing agreements which embrace a just-in-time policy not available if head office arranged purchasing on a group basis (or vice-versa).
- The degree of autonomy will influence the extent to which some functions are centralised and charged to Spiro Division from head office on some apportioned basis. The level of such charges and the basis of apportionment used will affect the absolute profit reported at Spiro Division.

(Other examples would be accepted).

(b) In order that corporate profit maximising decisions take place it is desirable that management at divisions are able to make decisions which take into account all relevant internal and external circumstances.

The 'general rule' of transfer pricing states that transfer prices should be set at marginal (variable) cost plus opportunity cost to the group. Where the general rule is correctly applied, any decision made with regard to internal transfer versus external sale or internal purchase versus external sourcing should lead naturally to the best decision from the corporate viewpoint on financial grounds.

For example, consider where division A can sell component X externally at £15 (variable cost £8) and has no spare capacity and division B can purchase component X externally at £12. Division B should purchase externally and division A should sell externally in order that corporate profit is maximised. If division A transfers to division B in this situation, a contribution of £7 is being foregone by the group on each unit of external sale (the opportunity cost to the group).

Consider, however, where divison A has spare capacity with which to provide units of component X for division B. In this situation there is no opportunity foregone by internal transfer and the transfer price should be set at £8 (i.e. variable cost). In this situation division B will purchase from division A rather than buy externally at £12 and group profit will be improved.

(Other examples would be accepted).

			Marks	Marks
1	**(a)**	Input to each process (3 × 0·5)	1·5	
		raw material cost	1	
		labour cost	1	
		overhead cost	1	
		WIP. per unit	1·5	6
	(b)	Current vs control standard		
		process losses and reasons	2	
		material input and reasons	2	
		net labour hours and reasons	2	
		labour idle time and reasons	2	
		overheads and reasons	2	9 (max.)
		(1 mark for identification/quantification and 1 mark for reasons)		
	(c)	ABC/TQM standard – identification AND comment in TQM context in relation to:		
		process losses	3	
		material	3	
		labour	3	
		overhead	3	12
	(d)	Comments and examples on range of additional control information (on merit)		8
				35
2	**(a)**	Fare revenue:		
		use of correct journeys	1	
		use of correct percentages	0·5	
		use of correct prices	3	
		advertising revenue	0·5	
		variable cost	1	
		fixed cost	0·5	
		overall presentation and totals	0·5	7
	(b)	Comments on data table and information (on merit)		6
	(c)	(i) combined probability schedule	4	
		profit or loss schedule	4	8
		(ii) EV profit		2
		(iii) cumulative probability of profit greater than £30,000		2
	(d)	for method (on merit) up to	3	
		correct figures	3	6
	(e)	Spreadsheet use (on merit) (2 × 2)		4
				35

				Marks	Marks
3	**(a)**	(i)	operating statements:		
			traditional basis	2	
			ABB basis	4	6
		(ii)	advantages and discussion (4 × 3)		12
		(iii)	activity change + comments	2	
			cost analysis by expense type for each activity	2	
			cost driver info.	2	
			root causes of cost drivers	2	8
			(allow marks on merit for other relevant comment)		
	(b)		ABC unit cost:		
			product design	2	
			purchasing	2	
			production	1	
			depreciation	2	
			packing	1	
			distribution	1	9
					35

			Marks
4	**(a)**	performance measures and comment (5 × 2)	10
	(b)	discussion (on merit)	5
			15

			Marks
5	**(a)**	discussion and relevant costs (4 × 2·5)	10
	(b)	relevant comments and examples including timescale (2 × 2·5)	5
			15

				Marks	Marks
6	**(a)**	(i)	statement construction (on merit)		4
		(ii)	discussion of autonomy on:		
			external sales/internal transfer mix	1·5	
			transfer price impact:		
			– on revenue	1·5	
			– on input costs	1·5	
			cost levels	1·5	6
	(b)		'general rule' philosophy	2	
			relevant examples	3	5
					15

Module E – Professional Stage

Accounting and Audit Practice (Scots)

December 1996

Question Paper:	
Time allowed	3 hours
This paper is divided into two sections	
Section A	TWO questions ONLY to be answered
Section B	BOTH questions are compulsory and MUST be answered

Section A – TWO questions ONLY to be attempted

1 Playmore plc acquired 60% of the ordinary share capital of School Ltd on 1 October 1996. The purchase cost of the shares was satisfied by issuing 200,000 ordinary £1 shares of Playmore plc at £1·75 per share. Issue costs of £20,000 were incurred. The companies' financial statements for the year ended 30 November 1996 were as follows:

Balance sheets at 30 November 1996

	£000 *Playmore plc*	£000 *School Ltd*
Tangible fixed assets	700	140
Investment in School Ltd	350	—
	1,050	140
Current assets		
Stock	60	180
Debtors	95	85
Cash	75	45
	230	310
Creditors: amounts falling due within one year	(160)	(100)
Net current assets	70	210
Total assets less current liabilities	1,120	350
Creditors: amounts falling due after one year	(420)	(70)
	700	280
Ordinary £1 shares	300	40
Share premium account	150	60
Profit and loss reserve	250	180
	700	280

Profit and loss accounts for the year ended 30 November 1996

	£000 *Playmore plc*	£000 *School Ltd*
Turnover	1,260	708
Cost of sales	(644)	(426)
Gross profit	616	282
Distribution costs	(248)	(42)
Administrative expenses	(130)	(84)
Operating profit	238	156
Interest payable	(28)	(12)
Income from School Ltd	18	—
Profit before taxation	228	144
Tax on profit	(113)	(54)
Profit after taxation	115	90
Dividends paid	(15)	(30)
Retained profit for year	100	60

The following information is relevant to the preparation of the group financial statements.

(a) At the date of acquisition the value of the tangible fixed assets of School Ltd at open market price was £200,000. The estimated net realisable value of these assets was £160,000. Because of the proximity of the acquisition to the financial year end, no depreciation adjustment is to be made in the group accounts, and the carrying value of the tangible fixed assets in School Ltd's accounts at the date of acquisition is deemed to be the year end value. All other assets and liabilities of School Ltd were stated at their fair values at the time of acquisition.

(b) The issue costs of £20,000 incurred on the issue of ordinary share capital had been charged to the profit and loss account of Playmore plc under the heading of 'Administrative expenses'.

(c) School Ltd paid an ordinary dividend of 10p per share on 1 November 1996. No further dividends were declared for the year ending 30 November 1996. ACT on the dividends paid in the year had been accounted for by both companies.

[P.T.O.

(d) Goodwill arising on acquisition is to be amortised against the profit and loss account over a six year period on the straight-line basis. A full years charge is to be included in administrative expenses for the year ending 30 November 1996.

(e) There were no intercompany transactions during the financial year and it is assumed that the profit of School Ltd accrues evenly over the year. School Ltd had not issued any shares since the acquisition by Playmore plc.

(f) The company's policy is to account for preacquisition dividends by treating them as a return of the cost of the investment in the subsidiary.

Required:

(a) Prepare a consolidated balance sheet and profit and loss account for the Playmore Group plc for the year ending 30 November 1996. (Notes to the accounts are not required: workings should be to the nearest £000.) (21 marks)

(b) Explain how the fair value might be estimated where the purchase consideration is in the form of share capital and no suitable market price exists (for example where the shares issued are those of an unquoted company). (4 marks)

(25 marks)

2 The following financial statements relate to Globelink International plc for the year ended 30 November 1996.

Group profit and loss account for the year ended 30 November 1996

	£000	£000
TURNOVER		
Continuing operations		
Ongoing	214,277	
Acquisitions	7,573	
	221,850	
Discontinued operations	54,853	
		276,703
Cost of sales		(220,398)
Gross profit		56,305
Distribution costs	21,886	
Administrative expenses	21,421	
		(43,307)
		12,998
Other operating income		894
Income from interests in associated undertakings		3,575
OPERATING PROFIT		
Continuing operations		
Ongoing	16,590	
Acquisitions	1,585	
	18,175	
Discontinued operations	(708)	
		17,467
Profit on disposal of fixed assets	1,170	
Discontinued operations:		
Loss on sale of operations	(3,168)	
		(1,998)
		15,469

[P.T.O.

	£000	£000
Income from investments	1,648	
Interest payable	(1,432)	
		216
PROFIT ON ORDINARY ACTIVITIES BEFORE TAXATION		15,685
Tax on profit on ordinary activities		(4,747)
PROFIT ON ORDINARY ACTIVITIES AFTER TAXATION		10,938
Minority interests		(404)
PROFIT ATTRIBUTABLE TO MEMBERS OF THE PARENT COMPANY		10,534
Dividends		(2,815)
RETAINED PROFIT FOR THE YEAR		7,719

Group balance sheet at 30 November 1996

	£000
FIXED ASSETS	
Intangible assets	2,680
Tangible assets	43,940
Investments in associated undertakings	26,670
	73,290
CURRENT ASSETS	
Stock	33,962
Debtors	26,470
Cash at bank and in hand	11,468
	71,900
CREDITORS: *amounts falling due within one year*	(32,530)
NET CURRENT ASSETS	39,370
TOTAL ASSETS LESS CURRENT LIABILITIES	112,660
CREDITORS: *amounts falling due after more than one year*	(16,338)

	£000
ACCRUALS AND DEFERRED INCOME	
Deferred government grants	(3,530)
MINORITY INTERESTS	(812)
	91,980
CAPITAL AND RESERVES	
Called up share capital	39,600
Share premium account	645
Revaluation reserve	12,725
Profit and loss account	39,010
	91,980

The following information is relevant to the financial statements of Globelink International plc.

(a) The group manufactures and sells printing machinery within the United Kingdom and Asia.

(i) Sales to Asian customers account for 32% of total group turnover.

(ii) Sales originating from Asian subsidiaries account for 34% of the total group turnover including intercompany sales.

(iii) Discontinued activities totally relate to United Kingdom business and operations.

(iv) Items (i) and (ii) above relate solely to continuing activities.

(b) Total intercompany sales from continuing activities were £16·5 million during the year. Asian subsidiary companies originated 20% of these sales.

(c) Asian subsidiaries contributed 24% of the continuing operating profit before taking into account common costs and the profit before tax of associated undertakings. Any apportionment of the common costs of £2·4 million was deemed to be misleading by the directors and therefore no apportionment was to take place. The associated undertakings are all operating from the United Kingdom.

(d) The group has 25% of its tangible and intangible fixed assets located in Asia and 30% of its current assets. No government grants have been received in Asia. The creditors falling due after more than one year relate to a loan obtained by the UK parent company. Additionally, the directors felt that it was not possible to allocate 'creditors falling due within one year' of £7·8 million between the segments. After adjusting for this amount, 30% of the balance related to activities in Asia.

(e) The directors have decided that for the purpose of the disclosure requirements of FRS 3 'Reporting Financial Performance', the acquisitions in the year do not have a material impact on a business segment as they relate to UK operations. However they consider that the discontinued operations have a material impact on the UK operations.

Required:

(a) Prepare a segmental report by geographical area for Globelink International plc in accordance with SSAP 25 'Segmental Reporting', FRS 3 'Reporting Financial Performance' and the Companies Act 1985 as amended by Companies Act 1989. (All calculations should be to the nearest £000.) (21 marks)

(b) Briefly describe FOUR limitations of SSAP 25 'Segmental Reporting'. (4 marks)

(25 marks)

3 The existing standard on goodwill SSAP 22, 'Accounting for Goodwill' permits a choice in method in dealing with goodwill. Essentially, this choice is one of capitalisation as an asset and subsequent amortisation through the profit and loss account over its useful economic life, or immediate elimination of goodwill from the accounts by writing it off against a reserve. Thus it seems that an ideal treatment for goodwill does not exist and that any revision of the existing standard on goodwill will be of an arbitrary nature.

Required:

(a) Explain the main arguments for and against the two main methods of accounting for goodwill allowed in SSAP 22 'Accounting for Goodwill'. (12 marks)

(b) State whether the following reserves may be used by a company to immediately write off goodwill against them, briefly indicating any alternative uses of each reserve.

(i) Revaluation reserve

(ii) Share premium account

(iii) Capital redemption reserve. (5 marks)

(c) Discuss the accounting implications and the effect on realised profits where goodwill is immediately written off against reserves and not as a charge in the profit and loss account. (4 marks)

(d) Discuss the view that whether a single treatment for goodwill exists or not is irrelevant as the important factor is full disclosure of the accounting policy for goodwill adopted by the company. (4 marks)

(25 marks)

[P.T.O.

Section B – BOTH questions are compulsory and MUST be attempted

4 Abroad Ltd is a 100% owned subsidiary of Home plc, a UK based company. Abroad Ltd is located in a foreign country and was purchased on 1 November 1995. The financial statements of Abroad Ltd are drawn up in accordance with the local accounting regulations. The following translated profit and loss account related to Abroad Ltd for the year ended 31 October 1996.

Abroad Ltd

Profit and loss account for the year ended 31 October 1996

	£000	£000
Turnover		8,900
Cost of sales		(7,094)
Gross profit		1,806
Sales and distribution cost	(633)	
Motor lorry depreciation	(32)	
Administration and finance costs	(541)	
Interest received	161	
Interest paid	(172)	
		(1,217)
Profit before taxation		589
Taxation: Corporation tax	(20)	
Deferred taxation	(68)	
		(88)
Profit after taxation		501
Extraordinary profit	103	
Less taxation	(33)	
		70
Profit after tax and extraordinary items		571
Dividends paid and proposed		(52)
Retained profit for the year		519

The following notes are relevant to the above profit and loss account.

(a) The extraordinary profit comprises the following elements. The company had withdrawn from a contract to develop property. As a result, it was felt that there were costs to be incurred of £50,000 before taxation relief (32%). Additionally the company had made profits on the sale of a factory. This factory had not been used for production purposes for several years. The profit on the sale of the factory was calculated using depreciated historical cost of £85,000. The carrying value in the accounting records after a recent revaluation was £180,000. The tax charge provided for on this transaction was £49,000 under the law of the overseas country.

(b) Abroad Ltd has provided for deferred taxation using the full provision method at the taxation rate of 32%. The cumulative accelerated timing differences are £875,000. The company has the following projected timing differences over the next three years.

Year end	31.10.97	31.10.98	31.10.99
	£000	£000	£000
( ) = reversal	225	150	(550)

Assume UK corporation tax rate of 35% and group deferred tax considerations can be ignored.

(c) The closing stock of Abroad Ltd includes stock of £2 million held on consignment from suppliers. The main terms of the consignment agreement, which can be terminated by either side, are such that Abroad Ltd can return any or all of the stock to the supplier without any penalty and the price paid to the supplier when goods are sold will depend upon the current price list of the supplier. The opening stock held on consignment from the same supplier was £1·25 million. No other accounting entries had been made regarding this stock.

(d) Abroad Ltd had issued £2 million of 8% debenture stock on 1 November 1995. This stock is repayable on 31 October 1999 and costs of £12,000 were incurred. The issue costs and interest paid for the year were both included in the interest paid figure of £172,000 in Abroad Ltd's profit and loss account.

The auditors of Home plc have been asked to make the necessary adjustments to the financial statements in order to ensure that they comply with the UK Accounting Standards and the Companies Acts.

The Home Group plc has many overseas subsidiaries which are audited by local firms of accountants. Some of these firms of accountants are affiliated to the UK audit firm and some are not affiliated. Where an overseas accounting firm is affiliated to the UK audit firm a rigorous quality control exercise has been undertaken by both parties to the affiliation agreement.

Required:

(a) Prepare a revised profit and loss account for the year ended 31 October 1996 for Abroad Ltd in accordance with UK Accounting Standards and the Companies Acts. (14 marks)

(b) Describe the factors which an auditor should consider before acting as 'principal auditors' to a group such as Home Group plc. (6 marks)

(c) Explain the procedures which must be undertaken in order to assess the work of other auditors in the audit of group financial statements. (7 marks)

(d) Discuss whether the above assessment process would differ if the other auditors in a group were affiliated to the principal auditors. (3 marks)

(30 marks)

5 Mildrain plc operated a number of retail outlets. These outlets were mainly large retail stores which sold food, clothing, furniture and financial services. The management of Mildrain plc decided that the company should join the world-wide computer network system called the Internet. The main purpose of this move was to allow potential customers to access information about their financial services operations and obtain quotations for mortgages and insurance in addition to share dealing facilities.

At the final audit of Mildrain plc, an audit assistant noticed the following facts:

(i) There appeared to be material understatements of a creditor balance as compared with the supplier's statement. The company's largest supplier of furniture had allegedly issued credit notes through the Internet for apparent overcharging relating to goods purchased by Mildrain plc in the period.

(ii) There seemed to be a large increase in the number of clients who had purchased insurance policies or taken out mortgages with the company. At the year end, there was a material accrual for commission to be paid by insurance companies to the company.

(iii) In both of the above cases the only audit evidence available was hard copy evidence provided by the Internet and representations made by management.

The audit assistant pointed out the above matters to the audit senior who felt that the audit evidence already gathered was sufficient and that any costs of further work would outweigh the benefits to be obtained. The audit assistant disagreed with this view but was unsure as to how to proceed with the matter.

Required:

(a) Discuss the potential problems a company may face where it gives unrestricted access to employees to the Internet system. (4 marks)

(b) Describe the controls which a company should introduce in order to prevent unauthorised access to the Internet system. (4 marks)

(c) Discuss the validity of audit evidence collected from the Internet system. (4 marks)

(d) Describe the additional work which the auditor ought to carry out to substantiate the two audit exceptions noted by the audit assistant. (5 marks)

(e) Describe how the difference of opinion between the audit senior and audit assistant should be resolved. (3 marks)

(20 marks)

End of Question Paper

Answers

1 (a)

Playmore Group plc
Group balance sheet at 30 November 1996

Fixed assets	£000	£000
Intangible Assets		114
Tangible assets		900
		1,014
Current assets		
Stocks	240	
Debtors	180	
Cash at bank and in hand	120	
	540	
Creditors: amounts falling due within one year	(260)	
Net current assets		280
Total assets less current liabilities		1,294
Creditors: amounts falling due after more than one year		(490)
Minority interests – equity		(136)
		668
Capital and reserves		
Ordinary £1 shares		300
Share premium account		130
Profit and loss reserve		238
		668

Group profit and loss account for year ended 30 November 1996

Turnover	£000	£000
Continuing operations		
Ongoing	1,260	
acquisitions	118	
		1,378
Cost of sales		(715)
Gross profit		663
Distribution costs	255	
Administrative expenses (working 3)	147	
		(402)

	£000	£000
Operating profit – Continuing operations	235	
Acquisitions	26	
		261
Interest payable		(30)
Profit on ordinary activities before taxation		231
Taxation on profit on ordinary activities		(122)
Profit on ordinary activities after tax		109
Minority interests – equity (working 7)		(6)
		103
Dividends paid		(15)
		88

Workings in £000

Cost of control

Cost of investment	350	Ordinary sh cap	24
less preacqn div	(15)	Share premium	36
		Revaluation surplus	36
		Profit/loss a/c	102
		Goodwill	137
	335		335

Revaluation a/c

Cost of control	36	Revaluation surplus	60
Minority interest	24		
	60		60

Minority interest

Balance	136	Ordinary sh cap	16
		Share premium	24
		School Ltd	72
		Revaluation surplus	24
	136		136

Group reserves

Goodwilll written off	23	Balance	250
Preaqn div	15	School Ltd	6
Bal c/d	238	Issue costs	20
	276		276

School Ltd – Profit/loss account

Cost of Control	102	Profit/Loss Res	180
Minority Interest	72		
Group Res	6		
	180		180

Workings (£000)

(1) ***Fair value calculation – School Ltd***

Fixed assets – fair value (Market Value)	200
carrying value	(140)
Revaluation surplus	60

FRS 7 indicates that open market values should generally be used to value tangible fixed assets. Where fair value is based on market price, the net realisable value will be different because of the costs of realisation and the dealers margin. There does not seem to be any intention of the company to dispose of the tangible fixed assets, therefore it is unlikely that net realisable value will be used in the fair value exercise. However the fair value should not exceed the recoverable amount of the asset. Thus if candidates use net realisable value due credit will be given although FRS 7 by inference prefers open market value.

(2) *Transfer from profit/loss a/c to cost of control*

Prior years profits	60% of (180–60)	72
Current years profits	60% of 10/12 of 60	30
		102

(3) *Administrative expenses*

Playmore plc	130
School Ltd (2/12 of 84)	14
Goodwill written off	23
Issue costs to be written off against share premium a/c	(20)
	147

(4) *Share Premium account*

Playmore plc	150
Less issue costs	(20)
Group balance sheet	130

(5) *Preacquisition dividend*

Dividend paid to Playmore plc by School Ltd	18
Preacquisition element	$10/12 \times 18 =$ 15

As Playmore has accounted for the whole of its share of the dividends, School must have paid its dividends after the date of acquisition. The tax credit on the dividends has not been accounted for by Playmore plc.

(6) *Group reserves*

Playmore plc at 1.12.95	150
Group profit and loss account	88
Group profit and loss reserves	238

(7) *Minority interests – Group profit and loss account*

Equity interest = $2/12 \times 90 \times 40\% =$ 6

(b) FRS 7 'Fair Values in Acquisition Accounting' recognises that it is not always possible to find a suitable market price for shares given as purchase consideration. This may be due to the fact that the shares are not quoted or if they are quoted the price is unreliable due to an inactive market. In this case the fair value should be estimated by looking at relevant information such as:

(i) the value of 'similar' shares that are quoted

(ii) the present value of the future cash flows of the shares

(iii) any cash alternative to the issue of shares

(iv) the value of any underlying security into which there is an option to convert.

If a value cannot be arrived at by any of the above methods, then a valuation of the company concerned should be undertaken.

2 (a)

Notes to the accounts at 30 November 1996

Segmental analysis – Globelink International plc

Geographical area	United Kingdom	Asia	Total
Turnover	£000	£000	£000
Turnover by destination:			
Sales to third parties			
Continuing	150,858	70,992	221,850
Discontinued	54,853	—	54,853
	205,711	70,992	276,703
Turnover by origin			
Continuing operations:			
Total sales	157,311	81,039	238,350
Intersegment sales	(13,200)	(3,300)	(16,500)
Sales to third parties	144,111	77,739	221,850
Discontinued operations	54,853	—	54,853
	198,964	77,739	276,703
Profit			
Segment profit:			
Continuing operations	12,920	4,080	17,000
Discontinued operations	(708)	—	(708)
	12,212	4,080	16,292
Common costs			(2,400)
Profits before tax of associated undertakings	3,575	—	3,575
Operating profit			17,467
Non-operating items			(1,998)
Interest payable and income from investments			216
Profit on ordinary activities before taxation			15,685
Net assets			
Net assets by segment:			
Continuing operations (see working 1)	48,116	25,806	73,922
Unallocated liabilities			(7,800)
			66,122
Net assets of associated undertaking	26,670	—	26,670
			92,792
Minority interest			(812)
Total net assets			91,980

Candidates will be given credit for alternative presentations of the above information.

As the associated undertakings net assets are greater than 20% of the groups net assets and results, the entity's share of the results and net assets of the associate have to be segmentally analysed. There is insufficient information in the question to classify operating and non operating assets.

Working 1	UK £000	Asia £000	Total £000	Apportionment
Intangible assets	2,010	670	2,680	75:25
Tangible assets	32,955	10,985	43,940	75:25
Current assets	50,330	21,570	71,900	70:30
Creditors within one year (32,530–7,800)	(17,311)	(7,419)	(24,730)	70:30
Creditors more than one year	(16,338)	—	(16,338)	—
Deferred government grants	(3,530)	—	(3,530)	
	48,116	25,806	73,922	

(b) *The following areas may be described as the limitations of SSAP 25*

(i) The determination of a company's classes of business is dependent upon the judgement of the directors. This lack of definition of business segments can lead to lack of consistency and comparability between the information disclosed by companies.

(ii) The basis of transfer pricing between group companies does not need to be disclosed. The absence of such information limits the usefulness of the disclosure of segmental results as it is possible to manipulate the profitability of segments by the use of intra group pricing strategies.

(iii) The standard allows common costs to be allocated to different segments on whatever basis the management of a company feels is reasonable. This can lead to an arbitrary allocation of such costs and again distortion in reported segmental results.

(iv) The standard does not give guidance on how to treat 'exceptional' items. By implication these items should be analysed between segments. In practice some companies analyse their results before exceptional items and do not always disclose to which segments they belong.

(v) Changes in the composition of the group and their effect on the segmental results are not dealt with by SSAP 25. FRS 3, however, requires that 'where an acquisition, or sale or termination has a material impact on a major business segment this should be disclosed and explained'. A revision of the detailed disclosure requirements in this area would produce more consistency of treatment.

(vi) Net assets are not defined for disclosure purposes by the standard although it does indicate that these will normally be non-interest bearing net assets. The standard does not explicitly say that the net assets figure to be disclosed is to be based on the year end position and some companies have used the average position during the year.

(Only four of the above limitations were required).

3 (a) The main arguments for capitalisation of goodwill as an asset and its subsequent amortisation through the profit and loss account are as follows:

(i) International comparability – this method is required practice in many overseas countries although requirements differ from country to country over the maximum length of life of goodwill.

(ii) This method is relatively straightforward to apply although the useful economic life of goodwill would need to be estimated.

(iii) It would be consistent with company law which requires goodwill to be depreciated over a period chosen by the directors that does not exceed its useful economic life.

(iv) The amount paid for goodwill represents an asset and it should be recognised as such on acquisition. Purchased goodwill diminishes in value over time and is replaced by internally generated goodwill. The loss in value of the original purchased goodwill should therefore be recorded in the financial statements as amortisation.

(v) Goodwill is an asset which has been purchased for the right to 'future economic benefits'. If this is the case then this method is consistent with the Statement of Principles as it satisfies the definition of an asset. However it is important that the goodwill figure be reviewed annually to determine if the figure represents 'future economic benefits'.

The main arguments against capitalisation and amortisation are as follows:

(i) As non-purchased goodwill is not recognised in financial statements, this method would cause problems of inconsistency when comparing the accounts of a group that had generated goodwill internally with a group with purchased goodwill.

(ii) The method does not provide consistency of treatment with the way the investment is treated in the accounts of the parent company. The cost of the investment in the parent company is only written down when a permanent diminution in value occurs. There is no automatic amortisation of the cost of the investment.

(iii) It is difficult to estimate the useful economic life of goodwill accurately and so the annual amortisation charges may be arbitrary.

(iv) If a company spends heavily in order to maintain or enhance the value of goodwill then this method results in two charges to the profit and loss account. One charge for the amortisation of goodwill and another for the costs of maintaining goodwill.

(v) It is often thought that this method understates the capital base of the company as the annual amortisation charge may not reflect an actual loss in value.

The main arguments for elimination of goodwill against reserves are as follows:

(i) This method is consistent with the treatment of internally generated goodwill as the latter is not recognised in the balance sheet. (In the profit and loss account, the treatment of the two kinds of goodwill remain different as the costs related to internally generated goodwill are charged whereas purchased goodwill is not charged under this method.)

(ii) The method is extremely simple. Once purchased goodwill has been eliminated there is no further accounting required except on a disposal or closure of a business.

(iii) This method is very popular in the UK because it does not have the perceived disadvantage of charging an annual amount to the profit and loss account regardless of the 'true' value of purchased goodwill.

(iv) Some observers feel that goodwill is not an asset but a once only expense associated with the acquisition of a company. Goodwill would be of no value, it is argued, in the event of a liquidation.

The following are arguments against elimination of goodwill against reserves:

(i) This method does not link the accounting for purchased goodwill with accounting for the investment in the parent company's accounts.

(ii) The reserves of the group can be significantly eroded. This will lead to a low value for net assets in the balance sheet and an incorrect assessment of the return on capital employed. The income of the group will be enhanced by the acquisition whilst the reserves will be reduced. Hence high returns on capital employed will result and this may mislead the uninformed user.

(iii) There is no 'accountability' in the group accounts for purchased goodwill since it is written off against reserves. No attempt to match costs and revenues is made.

(iv) The method is inconsistent generally with international practice. This method is far less common than the 'amortisation' method.

(v) The argument that goodwill is worthless on a liquidation is not relevant where accounts are prepared on a going concern basis.

(b) **(i)** *Revaluation reserve*

Revaluation reserve is a statutory reserve and the Companies Act 1989 states that such reserves can only be reduced by way of capitalisation. In this context capitalisation means applying the amount in wholly or partly paying up shares in the company. The revaluation reserve must be reduced to the extent that amounts standing to the credit of the reserve are no longer necessary for the valuation method used. (For example where a company disposes of an asset which has been revalued.) Thus the revaluation reserve is not available for the elimination of goodwill. Prior to the Companies Act 1989, it was possible to write off goodwill against revaluation reserve.

(ii) *Share premium account*

Share premium account is again a statutory reserve and cannot be used for writing off goodwill. It may be used for issuing bonus shares, writing off preliminary expenses or expenses of issuing shares or debentures or providing for the premium payable on redemption of debentures and redeemable preference shares. However, a practice has arisen in the United Kingdom whereby companies apply to the court to have the share premium account cancelled (under the terms of the Companies Act dealing with reduction of capital) and another reserve substituted for it. Restrictions on the distributability of the new reserve may be imposed by the court but normally goodwill can be written off against it.

(iii) *Capital redemption reserve*

This reserve is again a statutory one. It may only be used to pay bonus shares to shareholders. Therefore it cannot be used to write off goodwill although there appears to be no apparent reason why companies should not apply to the court to have another reserve substituted for it in the same way as previously described for the share premium account.

(c) The effect on 'realised profits' where goodwill is written off against reserves is dealt with in Appendix 2 to SSAP 22. The appendix makes it clear that the question is often irrelevant because the rules relating to distributions in the Companies Act relate to individual company accounts whereas most goodwill is written off only on consolidation. However, goodwill can also arise in the financial statements of an individual company where it acquires an unincorporated enterprise. Where goodwill is eliminated against reserves, a question arises as to whether realised reserves have been reduced. Where the value of goodwill has been permanently impaired, then the write off will reduce realised reserves.

However, the fact that goodwill has been written off against reserves does not mean necessarily that there has been a permanent reduction in value. The reason for taking goodwill to reserves in this manner is usually one of accounting policy. If the goodwill is written off because of an accounting policy, the realised reserves should not immediately be reduced. The reason behind this is that the purpose of the write off is one of excluding goodwill from the balance sheet and not to recognise that loss has been suffered.

Goodwill does not have an infinite life and therefore in this latter case, if the goodwill has been written off against an unrealised reserve, it may be appropriate to transfer an annual amount from profit and loss account to that reserve in order to simulate the effect which would have occurred if the company had chosen the amortisation method of writing off goodwill. The elimination of goodwill must be regarded as having reflected a realised loss. Such an accounting treatment involves estimating the economic life of goodwill and one of the reasons for using immediate write off against reserves is the fact that such an estimate is not easily made.

It is possible, in the case of a public company, that the goodwill write off to reserves can affect the company's distributable reserves, although it might have no impact on its realised reserves. This arises because of the restriction on distributions for public companies which prevent their net assets from being reduced below their share capital and non-distributable reserves. If the goodwill written off exceeds the unrealised profits and distributable reserves, then this restriction will apply.

(d) It can be argued that as long as the accounting policy for goodwill adopted by a company is disclosed in sufficient detail in the notes to the financial statements, then the sophisticated users of financial statements can adjust them to suit their own preferences. However, if there are alternative treatments for goodwill, then certain problems will always exist:

(i) Sophisticated users may be able to attempt to adjust financial statements for differences in accounting policy but often this will be difficult because of a lack of specific detail in accounts.

(ii) Unsophisticated users will not be able to amend the financial statements for differences in accounting policy and may be confused by the many accounting treatments. However, unsophisticated users should seek advice from sophisticated users on investment decisions.

(iii) National and international comparability of financial statements will be impaired if alternative treatments are allowed.

(iv) Historically companies have produced different versions/interpretations of the different accounting treatments allowed for goodwill. This has produced in essence a multiplicity of accounting treatments which in turn has led to different interpretations being 'placed' upon company law. For example the creation of negative reserves, and the writing off of goodwill against share premium account (see previous answer).

If a single or 'ideal' policy for goodwill is determined, then the problems outlined above can to a great extent be eliminated. The legal implications of such a policy can be determined, comparability can be enhanced and the source of confusion for users eliminated.

4 (a)

Abroad Ltd

Profit and loss account for the year ended 31 October 1996

	£000	£000
Turnover – continuing operations		8,900
Cost of sales		(7,844)
Gross profit		1,056
Distribution costs	665	
Administrative expenses	541	
		(1,206)
Operating loss		(150)
Provision for cost of withdrawal from property development	(50)	
Profit on disposal of tangible fixed assets	58	
		8
		(142)
Interest receivable	161	
Interest payable	(163)	
		(2)
Loss on ordinary activities before taxation		(144)
Taxation on ordinary activities		(109)
Loss on ordinary activities after taxation		(253)
Dividends paid and proposed		(52)
Retained loss for the year		(305)

Workings (all workings in £000)

1. *Cost of sales*

Balance in profit and loss account	7,094
Add consignment stock at 31.10.96	2,000
Less consignment stock at 31.10.95	(1,250)
	7,844

FRS5 'Reporting the Substance of Transactions' requires the above treatment of the consignment stock of Abroad Ltd.

It is likely that a prior year adjustment would be made if this accounting practice had occurred in the previous year.

2. *Exceptional items*

Provision for cost of withdrawal from property development		50
Sale of factory –	Sale proceeds (103 + 50 + 85)	238
	Less carrying value	(180)
Profit on disposal		58

3.

Year	Total Cost-PL/AC	Interest	Issue costs
1	163	160	3
2	163	160	3
3	163	160	3
4	163	160	3
	652	640	12

A straight-line method of writing off issue costs has been adopted on the grounds of materiality.

4. *Taxation*

Timing differences

	31.10.96	31.10.97	31.10.98	31.10.99
	875	225	150	(550)
Cumulative	875	1,100	1,250	700
Maximum reversal of 1996 timing difference		175		
(875–700)				
Rate of tax		32%		
Provision required		56		
Existing charge in profit and loss account		(68)		
Decrease in provision		(12)		

Tax charge in profit and loss account

Current charge	88
Decrease in deferred tax provision	(12)
Tax on 'extraordinary items'	33
	(109)

The opening provision at 1 November 1995 on the deferred taxation account of Abroad Ltd using the partial provision method would be zero. This can be determined by looking at the opeming timing differences which would be ($875 - 68 \times \frac{100}{32}$) i.e. 663 which means that there is no forseeable reversal.

(b) SAS 510 deals with the relationship between principal auditors and other auditors. In deciding whether to act as principal auditor, the auditors should consider whether they are participating sufficiently in the audit of the group to enable them to act as principal auditors. The factors they should consider when deciding are as follows:

(i) the materiality of the proportion of the group financial statements which they audit

(ii) the extent of the knowledge of the group's activities and structure

(iii) the closeness of their relationship with other group auditors

(iv) their ability to perform additional procedures regarding the quality of the work of other group auditors and at other group companies

(v) the risk of material misstatement of the elements not audited by themselves

(vi) whether the previous 'principal auditors' received their rights under the Companies Acts

(vii) whether 'professional clearance' had been obtained from the previous principal auditors

(viii) the independence of the audit firm regarding the group companies.

The purpose of the above factors is to determine whether the principal auditors are sufficiently involved with the group. If they are not sufficiently involved they should make stringent plans and efforts to become involved or not accept the appointment.

(c) At the planning stage of the audit the principal auditors should review the professional qualifications, experience and resources of the other auditors. This assessment will include the following factors:

(i) previous experience of their work

(ii) affiliation with other firms

(iii) membership of a recognised professional body

(iv) the principal auditors' impressions of the other auditors through meetings and discussions with them.

The principal auditors will also test the adequacy of the work of the other auditors. This will include discussing with the other auditors the reliance to be placed on their work and informing them of specific tests which need to be performed. Also the principal auditors should obtain representations concerning compliance with ethical standards and relevant auditing and regulatory requirements of the country concerned (if any).

A checklist or questionnaire can be completed by the other auditors to provide audit evidence or a review of the other auditors working papers may be carried out. The precise method will be determined by the principal auditors' evaluation of the quality of the other auditors' work.

The principal auditors will review the audit findings of the other auditors and any reports made to the management of the component of the group. As a result of the above procedures the principal auditor may decide that additional tests are necessary. These tests may be performed by the principal or other auditors depending upon the evaluation of the competence of the other auditors.

(d) Where the other auditors are affiliated to the principal auditors, the principal auditors will be more likely to rely upon the work of the other auditors without extensive evaluatory procedures being performed. The quality control procedures of a national or international association should ensure that the work performed by the affiliated firm will be of comparable standard to that of the principal auditors. The degree of reliance placed upon associate auditors' work will be much higher than that of an independent audit firm.

5 **(a)** Many companies are now offering services on the Internet. These services include limited banking facilities, mortgage advice, tax advice, share dealing and advertisement of company products. It is possible to buy and sell goods via the Internet. Thus an unauthorised official with access to the Internet could notionally:

(i) pay for goods of a personal nature by using a corporate credit card number

(ii) sell the company's assets

(iii) buy goods/services on behalf of the company

(iv) disseminate confidential information, for example, financial data

(v) give advice to customers which may prove to be negligent. The common practice of putting a disclaimer at the bottom of public messages is not a fail safe shield in this matter.

Obviously these possibilities are always likely in a company but the Internet gives staff more opportunity to carry out these acts. Thus an unauthorised official could cause significant disruption in the company's operations by gaining access to the Internet. The question as to whether the contracts made via the Internet in this fashion are legally binding is a separate question depending upon the circumstances of the case. However, it can be seen that access controls are essential to prevent problems being created by unauthorised access to this powerful medium.

(b) There are several controls which a company could use to prevent unauthorised access to the Internet system. Identity recognition procedures can restrict access to the system. Access may require the use of passwords, identity tokens or other security devices. Access controls will involve the use of a card, badge or key system, personal identification numbers (PINs) or a combination of these methods. These systems, however, control access and not the personnel. It is possible to gain unauthorised access to the system by using an authorised person's identity recognition device. Care must be taken to ensure that the system for issuing badges, keys, tokens or PINs is secure.

Systems may also operate by voice reference, fingerprint recognition, signature or other personal characteristics. Additionally it is normal for passwords to be encrypted in order to prevent unauthorised use of the password.

A physical control could be the removal of the relevant hard disk from the computer hardware. This would obviously prevent the user from gaining access to the Internet. Thus it can be seen from the above that it is important that the entry points to the system are shielded and protected.

Additionally procedural controls can be set up whereby information/transactions to be processed by the Internet are only dealt with by authorised personnel. Essentially there would be segregation of duties between the user department and the data input/output section. Also the company could set up a formal fraud/error control project. In a risk based analysis of the areas of corporate operations which are most at risk, the Internet system would obviously come under close scrutiny.

(c) Audit evidence assists auditors in their judgements concerning the relevance and reliability of the accounting assertions. It is the means by which the auditor achieves assurance about the reporting quality and is the basis for the auditors' opinion. Evidence should be valid and relevant. SAS 400 'Audit Evidence' says that the reliability of audit evidence can be judged by using certain criteria. These criteria are as follows:

(i) external evidence is more reliable than internal evidence

(ii) evidence from the company's records is more reliable when the internal controls are satisfactory

(iii) evidence obtained by the auditors is more reliable than that obtained from the entity

(iv) written evidence is more reliable than oral representations

(v) original documents are more reliable than photocopies or facsimiles.

Evidence collected from the Internet system could be valid audit evidence but the quality may vary. For example, a debtor could confirm a balance outstanding via the Internet using the debtor's ID. This could be construed as good audit evidence if there is no possibility for example of altering the debtor's reply. Again if the procedural controls over access to the Internet are good then the quality of the audit evidence derived from it is enhanced.

The auditor may set up his/her own access code on the Internet and test the information set up by the client on the Internet system. This audit evidence will then have some validity depending upon the quality of the client's initial input to the Internet system.

For example if mortgage quotations are made by the company via the Internet, the auditor could select a sample of these quotes as the base documents for his/her compliance tests. Evidence generated by the Internet can be printed out by the client and thus is in documentary form but the quality of the evidence will be determined by the validity of the source of the information.

(d) The additional work which ought to be carried out to substantiate the two audit exceptions are as follows.

Credit notes

A formal letter should be written to this creditor together with a detailed statement setting out the make-up of the outstanding balance in the client's records. The letter should ask for confirmation of the outstanding balance and/or a reconciliation of any difference between the amount in the creditor's records and that in the client's records. The reply should be sent directly to the auditors' offices. Additionally all the creditors' ledger should be scrutinised to see if there are any similar cases. If the auditor is suspicious then a creditors' circularisation should be performed and purchases cut-off further scrutinised and tests extended. Also the credit notes could be traced to specific purchase transactions/invoices and the truthfulness of the proposition that these were issued for overcharging can be examined.

The existing audit evidence can be further reviewed by looking at the Internet address from which the credit notes had been issued. The company should have a list of addresses of company suppliers and the source of the credit notes can be agreed to this listing.

Insurance policies and mortgages

A sample of the new clients who had taken out insurance policies and mortgages could be taken and direct confirmation techniques used to verify the authenticity of the transaction. Additionally the auditor could write to the insurance company or mortgage company stating the amount of the outstanding balance due to the client company and asking for direct confirmation of the balance outstanding to be sent to the auditor.

Again the auditor could look at the source address on the Internet for these transactions and try and determine the independent nature or otherwise of the audit evidence. Again the auditor could scrutinise this evidence for any related party involvement.

(e) Differences of opinion between members of an audit team are quite common because of the subjective nature of many of the judgements made by auditors. The matter should be resolved by open discussion between the members of the audit team and the audit senior should take responsibility for any decisions made. Audit assistants are often reluctant to express an opinion for fear of the affect it may have on their career. However, if the audit assistant is convinced that material error could occur there is an ethical obligation to bring this to the attention of the audit manager. The audit assistant may feel that a note disassociating himself from the decision should be placed on file. However, the decision as to the note's inclusion in the audit working papers will be made by the audit manager or partner and in reality, it is unlikely to be included in the file. The audit manager is likely either to disagree with the audit assistant in which case no note will be filed or agree with the assistant in which case additional work will be performed. The limited extent of an audit assistant's experience often leads to disproportionate significance being given to certain matters. However, in this particular case, it is likely that the audit manager will agree with the audit assistant and that the additional work will be performed.

Question 1

			Marks
(a)	Cost of control		6
	Revaluation to fair value		2
	Group reserves		5
	Minority interest		4
	School Ltd reserves		3
	Intangible assets		2
	Tangible assets		2
	Net current assets and creditors more than one year		2
	Share capital		1
	Share premium		2
	Turnover		2
	Cost of sales		2
	Distribution costs		2
	Administrative expenses		4
	Interest payable		2
	Taxation		2
	Minority interests		3
	Dividends paid		2
		Available	48 ÷ 2 = 24
		Maximum	21
(b)	Similar shares – quoted		1
	Present value of cash flows		1
	Cash alternative		1
	Value of underlying security		1
	Valuation of company		1
		Available	5
		Maximum	4
		Available	29
		Maximum	25

Question 2

			Marks
(a)	Turnover by destination		3
	Turnover by origin		3
	Segment profit		3
	Common costs		1
	Profit-associated undertakings		1
	Non-operating items		1
	Interest payable and income		1
	Net assets by segment		6
	Unallocated liabilities		1
	Net assets of associate		1
	Minority interest		1
	Unallocated liabilities		1
		Available	23
		Maximum	21
(b)	Classes of business		1
	Transfer pricing		1
	Common costs		1
	Exceptional items		1
	Changes in group		1
	Definition of net assets		1
		Available	6
		Maximum	4
		Total available	29
		Maximum	25

Question 3

		Marks
(a) Capitalisation and amortisation		
– arguments for 1 mark per point (max)		3
– arguments against 1 mark per point (max)		3
Immediate write off		
– arguments for 1 mark per point (max)		3
– arguments against 1 mark per point (max)		3
	Available/maximum	12
(b) Revaluation reserve		2
Share premium account		2
Capital redemption reserve		2
	Available	6
	Maximum	5
(c) Goodwill permanently impaired in value		2
Accounting policy		2
Discussion and effect on distributable profits		2
	Available	6
	Maximum	4
(d) Discussion – subjective assessment		4
	Available	28
	Maximum	25

Question 4

			Marks
(a)	Cost of sales		2
	Distribution costs		1
	Administrative expenses		1
	Exceptional items – property		2
	– fixed assets		3
	Interest payable		2
	Taxation		3
	Format		2
		Available	16
		Maximum	14
(b)	Sufficient participation		1
	Materiality of part audited		1
	Extent of knowledge of group activities		1
	Closeness of relationship with other auditors		1
	Ability to perform procedures		1
	Risk of misstatement		1
	Rights		1
	Professional clearance		1
	Independence		1
	Not accept appointment		1
		Available	10
		Maximum	6

		Marks
(c)	Professional qualifications	1
	Experience	1
	Resources	1
	Previous experience of work	1
	Affiliation	1
	Recognised body	1
	Impressions	1
	Adequacy of work	1
	Reliance to be placed	1
	Tests to be performed	1
	Representations re ethics and standards	1
	Checklist/questionnaire	1
	Review work	1
	Additional tests	1
	Available	14
	Maximum	7
(d)	Quality control	1
	No extensive tests	1
	Degree of reliance greater	1
	Available	3
	Maximum	3
	Available	43
	Maximum	30

Question 5

			Marks
(a)	Examples of potential unauthorised transactions		3
	Disruption		1
	Legality of transactions		1
	Access controls essential		1
		Available	6
		Maximum	4
(b)	Identity recognition procedures		2
	Physical controls		2
	Procedural controls		2
		Available	6
		Maximum	4
(c)	SAS 400 and reliability of audit evidence		2
	Discussion of validity of Internet evidence		3
		Available	5
		Maximum	4
(d)	Credit notes – additional work		3
	Insurance policies and mortgages		3
		Available	6
		Maximum	5
(e)	Discussion of process	Available	3
		Maximum	3
		Available	26
		Maximum	20

Module E – Professional Stage

Tax Planning

December 1996

Question Paper:	
Time allowed	3 hours
FOUR questions ONLY to be answered	
Tax rates and tables are on pages 66 to 68	

The following tax rates and allowances are to be used in answering the questions:

Income Tax

		%
Lower rate	£1 – £3,900	20
Basic rate	£3,901 – £25,500	24
Higher rate	£25,501 and above	40

Personal Allowances

	£
Personal allowance	3,765
Personal allowance – 65 – 74	4,910
Personal allowance – 75 and over	5,090
Married couple's allowance	1,790
Married couple's allowance – 65 – 74	3,115
Married couple's allowance – 75 and over	3,155
Income limit for age-related allowances	15,200
Additional personal allowance	1,790
Widow's bereavement allowance	1,790
Blind person's allowance	1,250

Car Fuel Scale Charge

	Petrol £	Diesel £
Engine Size		
1400cc or less	710	640
1401cc to 2000cc	890	640
2001cc and over	1,320	820

Mobile telephones

Cash equivalent of benefit	£200

Personal Pension Contribution Limits

Age	Maximum Percentage
Up to 35	17·5
36 – 45	20
46 – 50	25
51 – 55	30
56 – 60	35
61 or more	40

Subject to an earnings cap of £82,200

Capital allowances

	%
Plant and machinery Writing-down allowance	25
Industrial buildings allowance Writing-down allowance	4
Agricultural buildings allowance Writing-down allowance	4

Corporation Tax

inancial ear	Full rate %	Small companies rate %	Taper relief fraction	ACT fraction	Upper limit £	Lower limit £
991	33	25	1/50	25/75	1,250,000	250,000
992	33	25	1/50	25/75	1,250,000	250,000
993	33	25	1/50	22·5/77·5	1,250,000	250,000
994	33	25	1/50	20/80	1,500,000	300,000
995	33	25	1/50	20/80	1,500,000	300,000
996	33	24	9/400	20/80	1,500,000	300,000

Marginal Relief

$(M - P) \times I/P \times$ Tapering relief fraction

Value Added Tax

	£
Registration limit	47,000
Deregistration limit	45,000

Inheritance Tax

£1 – £200,000	Nil
Excess	40%

Rates of Interest

'Official rate' of interest: 10% (assumed)
Rate of interest on underpaid/overpaid tax: 10% (assumed)

Capital Gains Tax: Lease percentage table (extract)

Years	%
10	46·695
9	43·154
8	39·399
7	35·414
6	31·195

Retail Price Index

July	1991	133·8
January	1993	137·9
January	1995	146·0
December	1996	151·0
December	1997	155·0

Capital Gains Tax: Annual exemption

Individuals	£6,300

National Insurance (not contracted out rates)

		Rate	Lower limit £	Upper limit £
Class 1	Employee	10·0%[1]	61 p.w.	455 p.w.
	Employer	10·2%[2]	61 p.w.	–
Class 2		£6.05 per week.		
Class 4		6·0%	6,860 p.a.	23,660 p.a.

[1] Earnings below £61 p.w. are exempt; where earnings exceed this limit the first £61 per week is taxable at a reduced rate of 2%.

[2] Reduced rates apply in respect of low earnings, as follows:

Band

£		£	%
61	–	109·99	3
110	–	154·99	5
155	–	209·99	7

The amounts of dividends received or paid represent the actual amounts without any adjustment for tax credits or advance corporation tax.

Calculations and workings need only be made to the nearest £.
All apportionments may be made to the nearest month.
All workings should be shown.

FOUR questions ONLY to be attempted

1 ABC Ltd is an unquoted trading company that is under the control of three sisters, Agnes, Betty and Chloe, and is a close company. The share capital of ABC Ltd consists of 100,000 £1 ordinary shares, of which Agnes owns 20,000, Betty 40,000 and Chloe 40,000. Agnes and Betty are full-time working directors of the company, but Chloe is neither a director nor an employee.

Agnes is 57 years old, and is to retire on 31 December 1996. She will sell her 20,000 shares in ABC Ltd to Betty and Chloe for £20 per share. ABC Ltd's shares are currently worth £30 each for a minority shareholding. Agnes acquired her shares at their par value on 1 July 1991, the date of ABC Ltd's incorporation. She became a full-time working director of ABC Ltd on 1 July 1992. The market value of ABC Ltd's assets at 31 December 1996 is forecast to be as follows:

	£
Goodwill	500,000
Freehold property – factory and warehouse	1,050,000
Plant and machinery (costing more than £6,000 per item)	400,000
Investments in quoted companies	700,000
Motor cars	100,000
Current assets	750,000
	3,500,000

Agnes personally owns a freehold office building that is used rent free by ABC Ltd. This cost £78,000 on 1 January 1993, and is to be sold to Betty and Chloe for its current market value of £125,000 on 31 December 1996.

ABC Ltd will make an interest free loan of £200,000 to Chloe in order to help her finance the acquisitions from Agnes. This loan will be repaid over the next four years. ABC Ltd has an accounting date of 30 September, and is expected to have profits chargeable to corporation tax of £800,000 for the year ended 30 September 1997. No dividends will be paid during the year.

Agnes, Betty and Chloe are all 40% taxpayers. Agnes has not made any lifetime gifts of assets, and has an estate (excluding the above assets and the consideration to be paid by Betty and Chloe) valued at £400,000 which she has left to her children.

Required:

(a) Calculate Agnes' CGT liability for 1996–97. Your answer should include an explanation of the amount of retirement relief that will be available to Agnes. You should assume that holdover relief is *not claimed* in respect of the gift of business assets. (11 marks)

(b) Calculate the IHT liabilities that would arise if Agnes were to die on 30 June 1999. You should assume that the shareholding in ABC Ltd is still owned by Betty and Chloe at that date, and that the tax rates for 1996–97 apply throughout. (7 marks)

(c) Briefly advise both ABC Ltd and Chloe of the tax implications arising from the provision of the interest free loan of £200,000. (4 marks)

(d) As an alternative to Agnes selling her shareholding in ABC Ltd to Betty and Chloe, it has been suggested that the shareholding should instead be purchased by ABC Ltd for £20 per share. The purchase will not qualify for the special treatment applying to a company's purchase of its own shares, and will therefore be treated as a distribution.

Advise both ABC Ltd and Agnes of the tax implications arising from the company making a distribution. You are *not expected* to calculate ABC Ltd's corporation tax liability. (3 marks)

(25 marks)

2 (a) *"Every man is entitled if he can to order his affairs so that the tax attaching....is less than it otherwise would be". Duke of Westminister v CIR (1935).*

Required:

Briefly explain the difference between tax avoidance and tax evasion.
(2 marks)

(b) You are the tax adviser to Lucy Lee, who has been a self-employed architect for the previous 20 years. You should assume that today's date is 20 April 1997. Lucy has asked for your advice on the following matters:

(1) As a result of the transition to the current year basis, only one set of accounts has been prepared for the 24-month period to 31 March 1997, and these show a tax adjusted Schedule D case II profit of £285,000. The profit has been calculated after taking into account the following two changes:

(i) In previous years, Lucy has paid her employees a bonus on 31 March. This year the payment of the bonus, which amounts to £36,000, will instead be paid on 30 June 1997. No provision for this amount has been, or will be, made in the accounts to 31 March 1997.

(ii) On 30 April 1997 Lucy was due to complete a major contract for a client. However, at the request of the client, the contract was completed early on 25 March 1997. The fee for this contract is £57,000. Lucy accounts for fee income when a contract is completed.

Lucy wants to know whether the two changes will result in her Schedule D case II profits assessable in 1996–97 being subject to the anti-avoidance provisions that are applicable to this year, and the tax implications of the provisions being applied.

(2) From 1 April 1997 Lucy has employed her husband, who was previously unemployed, as a personal assistant at a salary of £28,000 p.a. This is more than Lucy's previous personal assistant was paid, but she considers this to be good tax planning. Lucy estimates that her Schedule D case II profit for the year ended 31 March 1998 will be £180,000. Her husband has no other income.

Lucy wants to know if employing her husband at a salary of £28,000 will result in an overall tax saving, and how such an arrangement will be viewed by the Inland Revenue.

(3) On 1 April 1997 Lucy set up a new business venture in partnership with her brother. The partnership designs building extensions for the general public at a fixed fee of £1,000 (including VAT). The forecast fee income is £35,000 p.a. A deposit of £500 is paid upon the commencement of each contract, which takes one month to complete. An invoice is then issued 21 days after the completion of the contract, with the balance of the contract price being due within a further 14 days. The partnership uses the office premises, equipment and employees of Lucy's architectural business.

(i) Lucy wants to know if the partnership will automatically have to account for VAT on its income as a result of her architectural business being registered for VAT.

(ii) Assuming that the new partnership *does* automatically have to account for VAT on its income, Lucy wants advice as to the basis that output VAT will have to be accounted for.

(4) Lucy's daughter is to get married on 25 May 1997, and Lucy is to make her a wedding gift of £12,500. Lucy's husband does not have any capital of his own, so Lucy is to make a gift of £12,500 to him on 24 May 1997 in order that he can make a similar wedding gift to the daughter. Neither Lucy nor her husband have made any lifetime transfers of value within the previous three years. Lucy wants to know the tax implications of such an arrangement.

Required:

Advise Lucy in respect of the matters that she has raised. You should assume that the tax rates and allowances for 1996–97 apply throughout.

You should note that marks for this part of the question will be allocated on the basis of:

6 marks to (1)
7 marks to (2)
6 marks to (3)
4 marks to (4) (23 marks)

(25 marks)

3 **(a)** Walter Smith, aged 59, is employed by Global Products plc as a sales manager. Walter is resident, ordinarily resident and domiciled in the UK. During the period from 1 October 1995 to 31 January 1997, Global Products plc sent Walter to three different overseas countries in order to set up new sales offices. His itinerary was as follows:

1 October 1995 to 30 April 1996	Working in the country of Arcadia.
1 May 1996 to 30 June 1996	On holiday in the UK.
1 July 1996 to 31 October 1996	Working in the country of Bellum.
1 November 1996 to 15 December 1996	On holiday in the UK.
16 December 1996 to 31 January 1997	Working in the country of Cadang.

From 1 February 1997 onwards, Walter worked in the UK. Global Products plc paid for all of Walter's travel and subsistence expenses whilst he was abroad. These amounted to £8,800, £4,100 and £2,500 for the trips to Arcadia, Bellum and Cadang respectively. The company also paid the travel expenses of £2,600 when Walter's wife visited him in Cadang during January 1997.

Walter is paid a salary of £36,500 p.a. by Global Products plc. His only other income is building society interest of £7,200 (net) p.a.

Required:

Calculate Walter's UK income tax liability for 1996–97. Your answer should include a detailed explanation as to whether or not Walter can claim a 100% deduction for a continuous 365 day qualifying period. You should ignore the fact that 1996 is a leap year in your calculations.

(12 marks)

(b) Walter is to retire on 6 April 1997. He will receive pensions of £19,500 p.a. Walter is to re-invest all of his building society savings overseas, and will receive the following income for 1997-98:

(1) Rental income of £8,500 (gross) from property situated in Arcadia. The rental income will be subject to Arcadian tax at the rate of 40%.

(2) Interest of £4,200 (gross) from Arcadia government stocks. The interest will be subject to Arcadian tax at the rate of 15%.

Required:

Calculate Walter's UK income tax liability for 1997–98. You should use the tax rates and allowances for 1996–97. (6 marks)

(c) In two years time, Walter and his wife are to leave the UK and are going to live in Arcadia. After leaving the UK, Walter will have the following chargeable assets:

	£
Assets situated in the UK	310,000
Assets situated in Arcadia	190,000
Total assets	500,000

If Walter were to die after moving to Arcadia, Arcadian death duty of £125,000 (500,000 at 25%) would be payable on his world-wide assets. There is no double taxation treaty between the UK and Arcadia. Walter has not made any lifetime transfers of value.

Required:

(i) **Advise Walter of when he will cease to be treated as domiciled in the UK for the purposes of IHT.** (3 marks)

(ii) **Calculate Walter's liability to UK IHT if he were to die after leaving the UK and (1) be treated as domiciled in the UK, or (2) be treated as not domiciled in the UK. You should use the IHT rates for 1996–97.** (4 marks)

(25 marks)

4 Jock and Maggie McHaggis are a married couple aged 36 and 38 respectively. Jock is a self-employed computer programmer, with annual tax adjusted Schedule D case II trading profits of £40,000. Of this figure, £34,000 relates to writing business software, whilst £6,000 relates to writing games software. The profits of £34,000 for writing business software are after taking into account capital allowances on Jock's private motor car, which currently has a tax written down value of £14,500. Jock drives 20,000 miles per year, of which 16,000 are for business purposes. None of the mileage is in respect of writing games software.

Jock owns 15,000 £1 ordinary shares in Lowloch plc. He inherited the shares on the death of his uncle, at which time they were worth £1.20 each. The shares are now worth £2.50 each. Lowloch plc pays annual dividends of 20 pence per share. Jock has deposits of £55,000 with the Ben & Burn Building Society, on which he receives interest at the rate of 7% p.a. (gross). His only outgoing is interest at the rate of 10% p.a. (gross) on a mortgage of £40,000. The mortgage is not within the MIRAS arrangements.

Maggie is employed as a saleswoman at an annual salary of £18,500. She has the use of a new 1600 cc company motor car with a list price of £11,500, and drives 20,000 business miles per year. No private fuel is provided.

A financial plan has been prepared for the couple that would reorganise their financial affairs as follows:

(1) A new limited company, McHaggis Ltd, will be formed, which will be wholly owned by Jock. The writing of business software will be undertaken by Jock for the company. Jock will still write games software on a self-employed basis. Jock will not receive any directors remuneration from the company, but will instead draw dividends of £2,000 per month.

Jock will continue to use his private motor car for business mileage. McHaggis Ltd will reimburse him for business mileage at the rate of 40 pence per mile for the first 4,000 miles, and 20 pence per mile thereafter. It should be assumed that these rates are the maximum allowed under the fixed profit car scheme.

(2) The maximum amount possible of the shares in Lowloch plc are to be held in personal equity plans. The remainder of the shares will be sold with the proceeds being invested in an income producing investment trust. The investment trust will produce a similar return to that from the shares in Lowloch plc. The relevant RPI factor in respect of the disposal is 0.390.

(3) The maximum amount possible of the building society deposits will be invested in a TESSA, which will pay interest at the rate of 7%. A further £20,000 will be used to repay a proportion of the mortgage. This is the maximum amount that Jock is prepared to repay off the mortgage at the present time.

Required:

(a) Advise Jock and Maggie of the income tax, CGT, corporation tax and NIC implications of the proposed financial plan. You should *ignore* the implications of VAT. Your answer should include:

(i) a calculation of the couple's taxable income before the financial plan is implemented,

(ii) a calculation of the tax saving that will result from each aspect of the financial plan. Your answer should be confined to the tax saving in the first year following the implementation of the financial plan,

(iii) advice as to any further tax planning measures that the couple should take, together with a calculation of the resulting tax saving. Your advice should be confined to the information given in the question, (20 marks)

(b) (i) advise Jock and Maggie as to where they could obtain independent financial advice, (2 marks)

(ii) briefly state whether or not you, as a qualified Certified Accountant, would need to be authorised to conduct investment business under the Financial Services Act 1986 in order to provide the financial advice given to Jock and Maggie. (3 marks)

(25 marks)

5 (a) You are the tax adviser to Alphabet Engineering, a three person partnership running an engineering business that commenced trading on 1 January 1995. Until 30 June 1996 the partnership consisted of Alfred, Bertie and Claude, with profits being shared in the ratio 5:3:2. On 30 June 1996 Claude resigned as a partner, and was replaced on 1 July 1996 by Daniel. The basis of profit sharing remained unchanged, with Daniel taking over Claude's profit share.

The partnership's tax adjusted Schedule D case I trading profit for the year ended 31 December 1995 was £122,000 (after capital allowances). The partnership's profit and loss account for the year ended 31 December 1996 is forecast to be as follows:

	£	£
Gross profit		420,000
Less: Administration expenses (all allowable)	253,600	
Depreciation	5,400	
Amortisation of lease	2,500	
		261,500
Net profit for the year		158,500

The partnership paid a premium of £25,000 for the grant of a 10 year lease on a workshop on 1 January 1995. The tax written-down value of plant and machinery at 31 December 1995 was as follows:

	£
Pooled assets	22,000
Partners' motor cars (owned by the partnership):	
Alfred – 40% private use	14,500
Bertie – 80% private use	8,000
Claude – 80% private use	15,000

Claude retained his motor car when he resigned from the partnership on 30 June 1996, at which date it was valued at £13,500. On 1 July 1996 Daniel introduced his private motor car into the partnership at a value of £10,000. The private use of this motor car is 70%.

The partnership's estimated tax adjusted Schedule D case I trading profit for the year ended 31 December 1997 is £190,000 (after capital allowances).

Required:

Advise the partners of the partnership profits that will be assessed on each of them for 1996–97. Your calculations should be made on a monthly basis. (12 marks)

(b) Alfred Letter, the senior partner of Alphabet Engineering, would like to start saving for his retirement. Alfred was born on 10 December 1958, and has not made any previous payments in respect of an entitlement to a pension. From 6 April 1989 to 31 December 1994 he was in employment at an annual salary of £36,000, but *was not* a member of an occupational pension scheme. Alfred is single, and has no other income or outgoings.

Required:

(i) **Calculate the maximum tax deductible contribution that Alfred could make into a personal pension scheme for 1996–97.** (5 marks)

(ii) **Briefly advise Alfred of whether or not it would be beneficial for him to actually contribute this maximum amount for 1996–97.** (4 marks)

(c) On 31 December 1997 Alphabet Engineering is to sell the lease on its leasehold workshop (see part (a)) for £45,000, and will purchase the freehold of another workshop for £65,000.

Required:

Advise the partners of Alphabet Engineering of the tax implications arising from the disposal of the leasehold workshop and the acquisition of the freehold workshop. (4 marks)

(25 marks)

6 Ongoing Ltd holds 80% of the ordinary share capital of Goodbye Ltd. Goodbye Ltd has faced deteriorating results in recent years, and therefore ceased trading on 31 December 1996. The company's recent results up to the date of its cessation are as follows:

	Adjusted D1 profit/ (loss) £	Schedule A £	Capital gain/ (loss) £	Franked investment income £	Patent royalty paid (gross) £	Deed of covenant paid to charity (gross) £	Dividends paid £
12 months to 30.9.92	88,500	6,000	(24,000)	–	(12,000)	–	–
12 months to 30.9.93	59,000	(1,100)	–	–	(12,000)	–	–
6 months to 31.3.94	62,500	2,600	–	17,500	(6,000)	(1,000)	–
12 months to 31.3.95	47,000	–	10,800	30,000	(12,000)	(1,000)	(46,000)
12 months to 31.3.96	(68,000)	–	–	47,500	(15,000)	(1,000)	–
9 months to 31.12.96	(250,000)	–	72,000	27,500	(11,250)	(1,000)	–

The rental income relates to one floor of Goodbye Ltd's office building that was let out until 31 March 1994. The dividend paid to Ongoing Ltd *was not* paid under a group income election.

The forecast results of Ongoing Ltd for the year ended 31 March 1997 are as follows:

	£
Adjusted Schedule D1 profit	93,000
Bank interest received	3,500
Debenture interest payable	(12,000)
Franked investment income – 20 June 1996	3,500
Foreign income dividend received (net) – 5 December 1996	1,800
Dividends paid – 15 May 1996	(86,000)
– 10 November 1996	(75,000)

As at 31 March 1996 Ongoing Ltd had unused trading losses of £14,500 and surplus ACT of £22,800. The dividend received and the foreign income dividend received are in respect of shareholdings of less than 5%.

On 1 April 1996 Ongoing Ltd acquired 60% of the ordinary share capital of Forward Ltd. All of the other shareholders in Forward Ltd have holdings of less than 5%. For the year ended 30 June 1996 Forward Ltd had tax adjusted Schedule D1 profits of £36,000, and is forecast to have tax adjusted Schedule D1 profits of £59,000 for the year ended 30 June 1997.

Required:

(a) Assuming that reliefs for trading losses are claimed in the most favourable manner:

(i) Calculate Goodbye Ltd's mainstream corporation tax liabilities for all of the accounting periods from 1 October 1991 to 31 December 1996. (9 marks)

(ii) Calculate the tax refunds that will be due to Goodbye Ltd as a result of the loss relief claims in respect of its trading losses for the year ended 31 March 1996 and the period ended 31 December 1996. You should ignore the possibility of any repayment supplement being due. (5 marks)

(b) (i) Calculate Ongoing Ltd's forecast surplus ACT as at 31 March 1997. You should assume that the maximum amount of group relief is claimed from Goodbye Ltd. (8 marks)

(ii) Briefly advise Ongoing Ltd of the alternative ways in which it could utilise the surplus ACT. (3 marks)

(25 marks)

End of Question Paper

Answers

1 (a) Agnes is over 50 years old, is a full-time working director of ABC Ltd, which is a trading company, and owns 5% or more of its ordinary share capital. She will therefore be entitled to retirement relief. The relief will be restricted:

(i) To a factor of 45% since Agnes has only been a full-time working director for four years and six months.

(ii) To the proportion of the gain represented by the ratio of ABC Ltd's chargeable business assets (500,000 + 1,050,000 + 400,000 = £1,950,000) to its total chargeable assets (1,950,000 + 700,000 = £2,650,000).

Retirement relief will also be available in respect of Agnes' disposal of the freehold office building since it is an associated disposal. The building has been let rent free to ABC Ltd, and is sold at the same time as her shareholding. The qualifying period will again be four years and six months.

Agnes' CGT liability for 1996-97 will be as follows:

		£	£
Capital gains arising on business assets			
Shareholding in ABC Ltd (working 1)			424,901
Retirement relief			
250,000 × 45%		112,500	
424,901 – 112,500 = 312,401 × 50%		156,201	
			268,701
			156,200
Freehold office building (working 2)		39,590	
Retirement relief			
1,000,000 × 45% =	450,000		
Less utilised	424,901		
	25,099 × 50%	12,549	27,041
			183,241
Capital gain arising on non-business assets			
Shareholding in ABC Ltd (working 1)			152,528
			335,769
Annual exemption			6,300
			329,469
Capital gains tax at 40%			131,788

Working 1 – Shareholding in ABC Ltd

Since Agnes, Betty and Chloe are connected persons, the market value of the shareholding in ABC Ltd will be used, rather than the sale proceeds.

	£
Deemed proceeds (20,000 × £30)	600,000
Cost	20,000
	580,000
Indexation 20,000 × $\frac{151.0 - 133.8}{133.8}$	2,571
Capital gain	577,429
Proportion relating to chargeable business assets	
577,429 × $\frac{1,950,000}{2,650,000}$	424,901
Proportion relating to chargeable non-business assets 577,429 – 424,901	152,528

Working 2 – Freehold office building

	£
Sale proceeds	125,000
Cost	78,000
	47,000
Indexation 78,000 × $\frac{151.0 - 137.9}{137.9}$	7,410
Capital gain	39,590

(b) *Potentially exempt transfer – 31 December 1996*

		£	£
Value transferred (600,000 – 400,000)			200,000
Business property relief:			
200,000 × $\frac{2,800,000}{3,500,000}$ (3,500,000 – 700,000) × 100%			160,000
			40,000
Annual exemptions	1996–97	3,000	
	1995–96	3,000	6,000
Chargeable transfer			34,000
IHT liability 34,000 at nil%			Nil

Estate at death – 30 June 1999

		£	£
Present value of estate			400,000
Consideration received (400,000 + 125,000)		525,000	
Less capital gains tax		131,788	393,212
Chargeable estate			793,212
IHT liability	200,000 – 34,000 = 166,000 at nil%		Nil
	793,212 – 166,000 = 627,212 at 40%		250,885
			250,885

(c) The loan of £200,000 is a loan to a participator since Chloe is neither a director or an employee of ABC Ltd. The company must make a payment of £50,000 (200,000 × 20/80) to the Inland Revenue being equivalent to ACT on the loan. This will be due on 30 June 1998, being nine months after the end of the accounting period in which the loan is to be made. Notional ACT will not be due on any part of the loan repaid before 30 June 1998. The notional ACT is not available for offset against ABC Ltd's corporation tax liability. When the loan is repaid, the notional ACT will be refunded, with the tax repayment being made nine months after the end of the accounting period in which the loan repayment occurs. There are no tax implications for Chloe unless part of the loan is written off.

(d) The amount of the distribution will be £380,000 (400,000 – 20,000). ABC Ltd will have to account for ACT of £95,000 (380,000 × 20/80), which it will be able to set-off in full against its corporation tax liability for the year ended 30 September 1997, since this is less than the maximum set-off of ACT for this year which is £160,000 (800,000 × 20%).

Agnes will be assessed on the grossed up distribution of £475,000 (380,000 × 100/80), and this will result in an additional income tax liability of £95,000 (475,000 × 40% = 190,000 – 95,000) for 1996–97.

2 (a) Tax avoidance involves the reduction of tax liabilities by the use of lawful means. The ambit within which tax avoidance can be applied is limited both by specific anti-avoidance legislation, and by the courts in relation to artificial arrangements to avoid tax.

Tax evasion involves the reduction of tax liabilities by illegal means.

(b) *Transitional year anti-avoidance measures*

Lucy's assessment for 1996–97 will be £142,500 (285,000 × 12/24), being the year of transition from the prior year basis to the current year basis. She is effectively only taxed on 50% of her profits for the 24-month period to 31 March 1997. There are therefore anti-avoidance provisions to prevent the manipulation of profits during the transitional period.

The provisions will apply where there is a change in business practice as to the timing of income or expenditure. Only changes to established practices will be caught by the anti-avoidance measures. The provisions will not apply to changes undertaken for commercial reasons.

(i) *Employees' bonus*

The practice of paying employees a bonus on 31 March is well established, and the change to 30 June 1997 is likely to be caught by the anti-avoidance measures unless there is a commercial reason for the change. Lucy has effectively shifted profits of £36,000 from 1997–98 to 1996–97.

(ii) *Completion of contract*

The contract appears to have been completed early for commercial reasons and is not likely to be caught by the anti-avoidance measures.

Lucy's 1996–97 assessment will be increased by £18,000 (36,000 × 50%). She will also be subject to a penalty unless details of the change are voluntarily disclosed.

Employment of Husband

Lucy's employment of her husband on a salary of £28,000 p.a. will reduce her income tax liability by £12,342 as follows:

	£
Salary paid	28,000
Employers class 1 NIC (28,000 at 10.2%)	2,856
	30,856
Income tax at 40%	12,342

There is no NIC saving as Lucy's Schedule D case II profits will still be in excess of the upper limit of £23,660.

Additional income tax and NIC of £10,628 will be due on the husband's salary as follows:

	£
Taxable income – Schedule E	28,000
Personal allowance	3,765
Taxable income	24,235

	£	£
Income tax: 3,900 at 20%		780
20,335 at 24%		4,880
		5,660
Employees Class 1 NIC		
61 × 52 at 2%	63	
394 × 52 at 10%	2,049	
		2,112
Employers Class 1 NIC		2,856
		10,628

Lucy's employment of her husband therefore results in an overall tax saving of £1,714 (12,342 – 10,628).

The salary paid to Lucy's husband will not be a deductible expense for Lucy unless it is incurred wholly and exclusively for business purposes. The salary will therefore have to be reasonable in relation to the duties performed by the husband. Since Lucy's husband is paid more than the previous personal assistant, the additional salary is likely to be disallowed unless it can be justified on the grounds that the husband has more duties than the previous personal assistant.

New business venture

For VAT purposes, the partnership is a separate taxable person from Lucy's architectural business which she runs as an individual. On this basis, the partnership would not be liable to register for VAT as its taxable supplies are below the VAT registration threshold of £47,000.

However, HM Customs and Excise can apply disaggregation rules if the partnership's business is effectively an extension of Lucy's architectural business. The partnership will then be classed as the same taxable person as Lucy, and would have to account for VAT on its income. The partnership is engaged in similar activities to Lucy, and is using her office premises, equipment and employees. It is therefore likely that the disaggregation rules will be applied.

Accounting for output VAT

The tax point for a supply of services is the earliest of (i) the date that the service is completed, or (ii) the date that an invoice is issued or payment is received. If an invoice is issued within 14 days of the service being completed, then this date replaces that in (i).

Output VAT of £74.47 (500 × 7/47) will be included on the VAT return for the period in which the deposit of £500 is received. The output VAT of £74.47 on the balance of the fee will be included on the VAT return for the period in which the contract is completed, since an invoice is not raised within 14 days. The VAT will be due within one month from the end of the relevant period.

Wedding gifts

Lucy's wedding gift of £12,500 will utilise her IHT annual exemptions of £3,000 for 1996–97 and 1997–98, and a further £5,000 will be exempt as a gift in consideration of marriage. The balance of £1,500 (12,500 – 6,000 – 5,000) will be a PET, and this will also be exempt if Lucy survives for seven years after the date of the gift.

Lucy's gift of £12,500 to her husband will be exempt from IHT as an inter-spouse transfer of assets, and the same reliefs will then be available in respect of his wedding gift. Such an arrangement could be classed as an associated operation, although the rules are unlikely to be applied in this situation. This assumes that the first gift is not conditional upon the second gift being made.

3 (a) Walter will be able to make a claim for a 100% deduction if he is abroad for a qualifying period of 365 continuous days. The two periods spent on holiday in the UK will count towards the 365 day period provided that they satisfy two tests:

(i) The period in the UK does not exceed 62 continuous days. This test is satisfied for both periods, since 1 May 1996 to 30 June 1996 is 61 days, and 1 November 1996 to 15 December 1996 is 45 days.

(ii) That the total time in the UK does not exceed one-sixth of the qualifying period to date.

The first period in the UK satisfies this test as follows:

1.10.95 to 30.4.96	Working overseas	212 days
1.5.96 to 30.6.96	On holiday in the UK	61 days
1.7.96 to 31.10.96	Working overseas	123 days
		396 days

The period in the UK is less than one-sixth of the qualifying period to date (396/6 = 66 days).

The second period in the UK does not satisfy the test:

Brought forward		396 days
1.11.96 to 15.12.96	On holiday in the UK	45 days
16.12.96 to 31.1.97	Working overseas	47 days
		488 days

The period in the UK to date (61 + 45 = 106 days) is greater than one-sixth of the qualifying period to date (488/6 = 81 days).

The period from 1 October 1995 to 31 October 1996 is therefore a continuous 365 day qualifying period, and a 100% deduction will be available against Walter's emoluments attributable to his overseas duties. For 1996–97 the deduction will be based on a total of 209 days, being the period from 6 April 1996 to 31 October 1996. Walter's income tax liability for 1996-97 is as follows:

	£	£
Schedule E – salary		36,500
100% deduction 36,500 × 209/365		20,900
		15,600
Schedule E – travel and subsistence (8,800 + 4,100 + 2,500 + 2,600)	18,000	
Allowable deductions	15,400	
		2,600
		18,200
Building society interest (7,200 × 100/80)		9,000
		27,200
Personal allowance		3,765
Taxable income		23,435

	£
Income tax:	
3,900 at 20%	780
10,535 (23,435 – 9,000 – 3,900) at 24%	2,528
9,000 at 20%	1,800
	5,108
Married couple's allowance (1,790 at 15%)	269
	4,839

A deduction is not available in respect of the travel costs of £2,600 for Walter's wife. This is because Walter was not working overseas in Cadang for a continuous period of at least 60 days.

(b) *Walter Smith – Income tax liability 1997–98*

	£	£
Schedule E – Pensions		19,500
Schedule D case V – Rental income		8,500
Schedule D case IV – Interest on government stocks		4,200
		32,200
Personal allowance		3,765
Taxable income		28,435
Income tax:		
3,900 at 20%		780
20,335 (28,435 – 4,200 – 3,900) at 24%		4,880
1,265 (25,500 – 3,900 – 20,335) at 20%		253
2,935 (4,200 – 1,265) at 40%		1,174
		7,087
Married couple's allowance (1,790 at 15%)		269
		6,818
Double taxation relief		
Interest on government stocks (4,200 × 15%)	630	
Rental income (working)	2,510	
		3,140
Tax payable		3,678

Working – Double taxation relief

The DTR on the rental income is the lower of:

(i) The overseas tax paid – 8,500 × 40% =		3,400
(ii) The UK tax on the overseas income.		
5,565 at 24% =	1,336	
2,935 at 40% =	1,174	
		2,510

Note: *The above calculation of DTR on the rental income of £2,510 is that expected from candidates. The strict statutory basis of comparing the income tax charged on total income, and income tax on that income excluding the rental income, results in DTR of £2,627.*

(c) (i) Domicile is a concept of general law and is not solely a taxation matter. Under general law, Walter will cease to be domiciled in the UK when he acquires another domicile of choice. This will require severing all ties with the UK, and settling in another country (Arcadia) with the intention of staying there indefinitely. Walter will have to demonstrate this intention by positive actions such as selling his home in the UK, and purchasing property in Arcadia. However, for IHT purposes Walter will be treated as domiciled in the UK for three years after ceasing to be domiciled in the UK under general law.

(ii) If Walter were to die and be treated as domiciled in the UK, he would be charged to IHT on his world-wide assets as follows:

		£
Chargeable estate		500,000
IHT liability	200,000 at nil%	Nil
	300,000 at 40%	120,000
		120,000
Double taxation relief (working)		45,600
		74,400

If Walter were to die and be treated as not domiciled in the UK, only his assets situated in the UK would be charged to IHT as follows:

		£
Chargeable estate		310,000
IHT liability	200,000 at nil%	Nil
	110,000 at 40%	44,000
		44,000

Working – Double taxation relief

The rate of IHT on Walter's estate is 24% (120,000/500,000 × 100).

On the assets situated in Arcadia, the DTR is the lower of the Arcadian tax paid of £47,500 (190,000 at 25%) and the UK IHT paid on those assets of £45,600 (190,000 at 24%). No DTR is given in respect of Walter's UK assets of £310,000. Relief may be given in Arcadia.

4 (a) *Taxable income*

The couple's present taxable income is as follows:

	Jock £	Maggie £
Schedule D case II	40,000	
Schedule E		18,500
Car benefit (11,500 × 35% × 1/3)		1,342
Dividends – Lowloch plc (15,000 × 20p × 100/80)	3,750	
BSI (55,000 at 7%)	3,850	
	47,600	19,842
Personal allowances	3,765	3,765
Taxable income	43,835	16,077

Formation of McHaggis Ltd

By transferring the writing of business software to McHaggis Ltd, class 4 NIC will no longer be payable. The profits of £6,000 relating to the writing of games software are below the class 4 NIC lower limit of £6,860. This is a tax saving of £1,008 ((23,660 – 6,860) at 6%). Class 2 NIC of £315 (6.05 × 52) will still be payable.

McHaggis Ltd's mainstream corporation tax liability will be £1,776 calculated as follows:

	£	£
Tax adjusted D case II profit per sole tradership		34,000
Add: Capital allowances no longer available 3,000 (maximum WDA) × 16,000/20,000		2,400
		36,400
Less: Mileage allowance 4,000 at 40 pence	1,600	
12,000 at 20 pence	2,400	
		4,000
PCTCT		32,400
Corporation tax at 24%		7,776
ACT (2,000 × 12 × 20/80)		6,000
MCT		1,776

The ACT is less than the maximum ACT set-off of £6,480 (32,400 at 20%).

Dividends/Mileage allowance

Following the implementation of the financial plan, Jock's software writing related income will remain at £40,000, but will consist of the following:

	£
Schedule D case II	6,000
Dividends from McHaggis Ltd (2,000 × 12 × 100/80)	30,000
Mileage allowance	4,000
	40,000

The mileage allowance will be tax-free as the rates are within the limits set by the fixed rate profit car scheme. This is an income tax saving of £1,600 (4,000 at 40%).

The extraction of profits by way of dividends will mean that neither employers nor employees class 1 NIC will be payable. Dividend income is taxable at the rate of 20%, so there is a further income tax saving of £864 ((25,500 – 3,900) at 4% (24 – 20)).

Disposal of shares in Lowloch plc

It is not normally possible to transfer shares directly into a PEP. Therefore, Jock will have to dispose of all 15,000 shares in Lowloch plc. This will result in a chargeable gain of £6,180 as follows:

	£
Sale proceeds (15,000 × 2.50)	37,500
Cost (15,000 × 1.20)	18,000
	19,500
Indexation 18,000 × 0.390	7,020
	12,480
Annual exemption	6,300
	6,180

Prior to the disposal, Jock should transfer 7,427 (15,000 × 6,180/12,480) of the shares in Lowloch plc to Maggie. The transfer will be at no gain/no loss, and will enable her annual exemption to be utilised. No CGT will then be payable.

Personal equity plans

The maximum investment in a PEP is £6,000 p.a., with a further investment of £3,000 being allowed in a single company (or corporate) PEP. It will therefore be possible for Jock and Maggie to invest a total of £18,000 ((6,000 + 3,000) × 2) in PEPs holding the ordinary shares of Lowloch plc. This assumes that Lowloch plc is incorporated in, and listed on a Stock Exchange in, the European Union, and is thus a qualifying investment. The dividend yield on the ordinary shares of Lowloch plc is 10% as follows:

$$\frac{20 \text{ pence}}{250 \text{ pence}} \times \frac{100}{1} \times \frac{100}{80} = 10\%$$

The dividend income from the PEPs of £1,800 (18,000 at 10%) will be tax-free which is an income tax saving of £720 (1,800 at 40%).

Investment trust

The investment in the income producing investment trust of £19,500 (37,500 – 18,000) will not result in any tax saving. It will, however, carry a lower level of risk compared to an investment in the shares of only one company such as Lowloch plc. Since the rate of return from the investment trust is similar to that from Lowloch plc Jock and Maggie would be advised to invest their general PEP allowances of £6,000 each in the investment trust rather than the ordinary shares in Lowloch plc. A single company PEP cannot be used to hold shares in an investment trust.

TESSAs

Both Jock and Maggie can open up a TESSA, with each of them being able to invest a maximum of £3,000 in the first year. The interest of £420 ((3,000 × 2) at 7%) will be tax-free, which is an income tax saving of £168 (420 at 40%).

Repayment of mortgage

The £20,000 repayment of Jock's mortgage will result in an income tax saving of £410 as follows:

		£	£
Building society interest foregone (20,000 at 7%)			1,400
Tax saving 1,400 at 40%			560
Less: Tax relief on mortgage interest no longer available	10,000 at nil%	Nil	
	10,000 at 15%	150	
			150
			410

Utilisation of Maggie's 24% tax band

Maggie is not utilising £9,423 (25,500 – 16,077) of her 24% tax band. Since all of Jock's income taxable at 40% is dividend or savings income, the potential annual income tax saving is £1,885 (9,423 × (40 – 20%)). The transfer of income from Jock to Maggie could be achieved by making Maggie a 31·4% (100% × 9,423/30,000) shareholder of McHaggis Ltd.

Overall tax saving

The overall annual tax saving from the implementation of the financial plan together with the further tax planning measures is £4,879 (1,008 – 1,776 + 1,600 + 864 + 720 + 168 + 410 + 1,885).

(b) (i) Financial advisers are classified into tied advisers and independent advisers. Tied advisers only recommend the investment products of one financial institution, and do not therefore provide independent financial advice. Generally, accountants, solicitors and stockbrokers are independent advisers, along with some banks and building societies. Independent advisers can recommend investment products from any source.

(ii) Unless the activities do not constitute the *carrying on of a business* (such as providing financial advice to a friend or relative who is not otherwise a client, and who will not be charged a fee), a qualified Certified Accountant would have to be authorised to conduct investment business under the Financial Services Act 1986 in order to give the advice to Jock and Maggie. This is because the definition of *investments* includes shares, PEPs and investment trusts (but not TESSAs and mortgages), and the definition of *investment activities* includes specific advice regarding the purchase or sale of investments.

5 **(a)** *Alphabet Engineering – Adjusted Schedule D case I profit for the year ended 31 December 1996*

		£	£
Net profit per accounts			158,500
Add:	Depreciation		5,400
	Amortisation of lease		2,500
			166,400
Less:	Capital allowances (working 1)	8,750	
	Lease deduction (working 2)	2,050	
			10,800
Schedule D case I profit			155,600

Divisible:	Alfred – 50%	77,800
	Bertie – 30%	46,680
	Claude – 20% × 6/12	15,560
	Daniel – 20% × 6/12	15,560

Partners' 1996-97 Schedule D case 1 assessments

Alfred (year ended 31.12.96)		77,800
Bertie (year ended 31.12.96)		46,680
Claude (1.1.96 to 30.6.96)	15,560	
Less: Overlap relief (working 3)	6,100	
		9,460
Daniel (Actual 1.7.96 to 5.4.97)		
1.7.96 to 31.12.96	15,560	
1.1.97 to 5.4.97 190,000 × 20% × 3/12	9,500	
		25,060

The cessation rules apply to Claude who resigned as a partner on 30 June 1996, and the commencement rules apply to Daniel who joined the partnership on 1 July 1996.

Working 1 – Capital allowances

Motor cars

	Pool	Alfred	Bertie	Claude		Daniel	Allowances
	£	£	£	£		£	£
WDV b/f	22,000	14,500	8,000	15,000			
Addition						10,000	
Deemed proceeds				13,500			
Balancing allowance				1,500	× 20%		300
WDA – 25%	5,500						5,500
WDA – Restricted		3,000	× 60%			1,800	
WDA – 25%			2,000	× 20%			400
WDA – 25%						2,500	× 30% 750
WDV c/f	16,500	11,500	6,000			7,500	8,750

Working 2 – Lease deduction

The proportion of the premium assessed on the owners will be deductible against the partnership's Schedule DI assessment over the period of the lease.

	£
Premium paid	25,000
Less: 25,000 × 2% × (10 – 1)	4,500
	20,500
20,500/10 =	2,050 p.a.

Working 3 – Overlap relief

Claude will have overlap profits for the period 1 January 1995 to 5 April 1995 as follows:

122,000 × 20% × 3/12 = £6,100

Tutorial note

Apportionment should strictly be made using days, but the nearest month has been used in the answer due to the inclusion of estimated figures in the question.

(b) **(i)** Alfred's maximum tax deductible personal pension contribution is £60,354 calculated as follows:

		Net relevant earnings £	Relevant percentage	Maximum premium £
1990–91	Schedule E	36,000	17·5	6,300
1991–92	Schedule E	36,000	17·5	6,300
1992–93	Schedule E	36,000	17·5	6,300
1993–94	Schedule E	36,000	17·5	6,300
1994–95	Schedule E			
	36,000 × 9/12	27,000		
	Schedule D (working)	15,250		
		42,250	17·5	7,394
1995–96	Schedule D (working)	61,000	20	12,200
1996–97	Schedule D	77,800	20	15,560
				60,354

Unused relief is carried forward for six years, and utilised on a FIFO basis.

Working – Schedule D assessments

	£
1994–95 (Actual 1.1.95 to 5.4.95) 122,000 × 50% × 3/12 =	15,2
1995–96 (Year ended 31.12.95) 122,000 × 50%	61,0

(ii) Alfred has sufficient Schedule D profits for 1996–97 to utilise a personal pens premium of £60,354, but it would be beneficial to limit the premium to earnings that are taxable at the rate of 40%. A premium of £48,535 sho therefore be paid for 1996–97, calculated as follows:

	£
Schedule D	77,8
Personal allowance	3,7
Taxable income	74,0
20/24% tax band	25,5
Taxable at 40%	48,5

The premium can either be paid during 1996–97 or, alternatively, could be p by 5 April 1998 with an election being made by Alfred to relate the premium b to 1996–97. The unused relief of £11,819 (60,354 – 48,535) can be utilised

(1) Paying a premium before 5 April 1997, and electing to relate it bac 1995–96.

(2) Carrying it forward and paying a premium in respect of 1997–98.

In either case, tax relief at the rate of 40% will be obtained.

(c) *Sale of leasehold workshop*

The disposal of the leasehold property will result in a capital gain as follows:

	£	£
Proceeds		45,
Cost $25{,}000 \times \frac{35{\cdot}414}{46{\cdot}695}$	18,960	
Less: Lease deductions 2,050 × 3	6,150	
		12,
		32,
Indexation 12,810 × $\frac{155{\cdot}0 - 146{\cdot}0}{146.0}$		
Capital gain		31,
Divisible: Alfred – 50%		15
Bertie – 30%		9
Daniel – 20%		6

Each partner will be assessed to his share of the capital gain for 1997 Alternatively, it will be possible for a partner to rollover his share of the gain ag his share of the cost of the freehold workshop, since all of the proceeds fron disposal of the leasehold workshop have been re-invested.

Note: The lease deduction is a specialised point, and is therefore treated as a bonus mark in the marking scheme.

Purchase of freehold workshop

Industrial buildings allowance of £2,600 p.a. (65,000 at 4%) will be available, commencing in the period of account during which the workshop is brought into use.

6 **(a) (i)**

Period ended	30.9.92	30.9.93	31.3.94	31.3.95	31.3.96	31.12.96
	£	£	£	£	£	£
D1 Profits	88,500	59,000	62,500	47,000		
Schedule A	6,000		2,600			
Schedule A loss b/f			(1,100)			
Capital gain				10,800		72,000
Capital loss b/f				(10,800)		(13,200)
	94,500	59,000	64,000	47,000	–	58,800
Less s.393A(1)						
Y/E 31.3.96			33,000	35,000		
P/E 31.12.96 (working 1)		23,500	25,000			58,800
	94,500	35,500	6,000	12,000	–	–
Patent royalty	12,000	12,000	6,000	12,000	–	–
	82,500	23,500	–	–	–	–
Deed of covenant			–	–	–	–
PCTCT	82,500	23,500	–	–	–	–
Corporation tax at 25%	20,625	5,875				
ACT carried back		2,000	(working 2)			
MCT	20,625	3,875				

Working 1 – s.393A(1) loss relief

The claim under s.393A(1) ICTA 1988 for the year ended 30 September 1993 is £47,000 (59,000 – 12,000) × 6/12 = £23,500. Alternative calculations of the claim would be acceptable.

Working 2 – ACT

	£	
Franked payment Y/E 31.3.95	57,500	(46,000 × 100/80)
FII Y/E 31.3.95	(30,000)	
FII b/f	(17,500)	
	10,000	
ACT at 20%	2,000	

(ii) As a result of the claims under s.393A(1) ICTA 1988 the following corporation tax refunds will be due:

Year ended 30.9.93	£7,875 due to loss relief (23,500 at 25% = £5,875) and ACT carried back (£2,000).
Period ended 31.3.94	£14,250 due to loss relief (58,000 – 1,000 at 25%).
Year ended 31.3.95	£6,500 due to loss relief (35,000 – 1,000 at 25% = £8,500 less ACT now surplus of £2,000).

Goodbye Ltd can also claim under s.242 ICTA 1988 to utilise the loss for the period ended 31 December 1996 against surplus franked investment income for the year ended 31 March 1996 and the period ended 31 December 1996. A refund of tax credits will be obtained as follows:

Year ended 31.3.96	£9,500 (47,500 at 20%).
Period ended 31.12.96	£5,500 (27,500 at 20%).

This claim will utilise losses of £75,000 (47,500 + 27,500).

(b) (i) As at 31 March 1997 Ongoing Ltd will have surplus ACT of £58,850 calculated as follows:

	£
Franked payment 15.5.96 (86,000 × 100/80)	107,500
Franked payment 10.11.96 (75,000 × 100/80)	93,750
	201,250
FII 20.6.96	3,500
	197,750
ACT at 20%	39,550
Surplus ACT b/f	22,800
	62,350
Maximum ACT set-off (working 1)	3,500
Surplus ACT	58,850

The foreign income dividend received cannot be offset against franked payments.

Working 1 – Maximum ACT set-off

Ongoing Ltd's profits chargeable to corporation tax for the year ended 31 March 1997 will be as follows:

	£
Schedule D1 Profit (93,000 – 12,000)	81,000
Less s.393(1)	14,500
	66,500
Schedule DIII	3,500
	70,000
Less s.402 (working 2)	52,500
PCTCT	17,500

The maximum ACT offset is £3,500 (17,500 at 20%).

Working 2 – Claim under s.402 ICTA 1988

Losses under s.402 ICTA 1988 can only be offset against profits of the corresponding period. Goodbye Ltd ceased trading on 31 December 1996 so the corresponding period is 1 April 1996 to 31 December 1996. The group relief claim is therefore limited to £52,500 (70,000 × 9/12). This is less than Goodbye Ltd's unrelieved losses available for group relief for the period ended 31 December 1996 of £79,950, calculated as follows:

	£
Schedule D1 trading loss	250,000
Utilised under s.393A(1) (58,800 + 25,000 + 23,500)	(107,300)
Utilised under s.242	(75,000)
	67,700
Excess charges (11,250 + 1,000)	12,250
	79,950

Tutorial note

The deed of covenant to charity of £1,000 is included in the unrelieved losses of £79,950 since non-trade charges can be group relieved.

(ii) Ongoing Ltd could utilise its surplus ACT as follows:

(1) The surplus ACT can be carried back and set against the corporation tax liability of accounting periods commencing in the previous six years. Since Ongoing Ltd has surplus ACT brought forward, it is unlikely that the carry back of surplus ACT is possible.

(2) The surplus ACT can be carried forward and set against the corporation tax liability of future accounting periods, subject to the maximum set-off limit.

(3) The surplus ACT can be surrendered to Forward Ltd as it is a 51% subsidiary. Only the current year ACT of £39,550 can be surrendered. This may be utilised by Forward Ltd against its corporation tax liability for the year ended 30 June 1997. Forward Ltd was not a 51% subsidiary throughout the year ended 30 June 1996. The maximum set-off will be £11,800 (59,000 at 20%).

This marking scheme is given as a guide to markers in the context of the suggested answer. Scope is given to markers to award marks for alternative approaches to a question, including relevant comment, and where well reasoned conclusions are provided. This is particularly the case for essay based questions where there will often be more than one definitive solution.

			Marks
1	**(a)**	*Retirement relief*	
		Qualifying conditions	1
		Restriction to 45%	1
		Restriction to chargeable business assets	1
		Associated disposal	2
		Calculation of CGT liability	
		Capital gain	1
		Proportion relating to chargeable business assets	1
		Retirement relief	1
		Gain on freehold office building	1
		Retirement relief on associated disposal	1
		Annual exemption/CGT	1
		Maximum/Available	11
	(b)	*Potentially exempt transfer*	
		Value transferred	1
		Business property relief	2
		Annual exemptions/IHT liability	1
		Estate at death	
		Capital gains tax deduction	1
		Calculation of IHT liability	2
		Maximum/Available	7
	(c)	Loan to participator	1
		Payment to the Inland Revenue	1
		Treatment of notional ACT/Repayment of loan	1
		Tax position of participator	1
		Maximum/Available	4
	(d)	ACT	2
		Assessment on shareholder	2
		Available	4
		Maximum	3
		Available	26
		Maximum	25

			Marks
2	(a)	Tax avoidance	1
		Tax evasion	1
		Maximum/Available	2
	(b)	*Transitional year anti-avoidance measures*	
		1996–97 assessment	1
		Anti-avoidance provisions	1
		Application of provisions	1
		Employees' bonus	2
		Completion of contract	1
		Penalties	1
		Employment of husband	
		Income tax saving – wife	2
		Additional income tax – husband	1
		Class 1 NIC	1
		Overall tax saving	1
		Deductibility of salary	1
		Disallowance of salary	1
		Justification of salary	1
		New business venture	
		Separate taxable person	1
		VAT registration	1
		Disaggregation rules	1
		Application of rules	1
		Accounting for output VAT	
		Tax point	1
		Output VAT on the deposit	1
		Output VAT on the balance	1
		Wedding gifts	
		Exemptions available	1
		Potentially exempt transfer	1
		Inter-spouse transfer	1
		Associated operation	2
		Available	27
		Maximum	23
		Available	29
		Maximum	25

			Marks
3	**(a)**	*365 day qualifying period*	
		100% deduction	1
		62 day test	1
		First period in UK	2
		Second period in UK	2
		Qualifying period	1
		Calculation of income tax liability	
		Salary/100% deduction	2
		Travel and subsistence	1
		BSI/Personal allowance	1
		Income tax liability/MCA	2
		Wife's travel expenses	1
		Available	14
		Maximum	12
	(b)	Taxable income	1
		Income tax liability/MCA	2
		DTR on government stocks	1
		DTR on rental income	2
		Maximum/Available	6
	(c)	**(i)** Domicile of choice	1
		Requirements	1
		IHT position	1
		Maximum/Available	3
		(ii) *Domiciled in UK*	
		Principle	1
		Calculation of IHT liability	1
		DTR on assets situated in Arcadia	1
		Not domiciled in UK	
		Principle	1
		Calculation of IHT liability	1
		Available	5
		Maximum	4
		Available	28
		Maximum	25

			Marks
4	**(a)**	Calculation of taxable income	2
		Formation of McHaggis Ltd	
		Class 4 NIC	1
		Tax saving	1
		Capital allowances adjustment	1
		Mileage allowance	1
		ACT	1
		Dividends/Mileage allowance	
		Calculation of income	1
		Mileage allowance	1
		Class 1 NIC	1
		Tax saving	1
		Disposal of shares in Lowloch plc	
		Transfer to a PEP	1
		Calculation of capital gain	1
		Tax planning	1
		Personal equity plans	
		Maximum investment	1
		Qualifying investment	1
		Dividend yield	1
		Tax saving	1
		Investment trust	
		Tax position/Level of risk	1
		Advice	1
		TESSAs	
		Maximum investment	1
		Tax saving	1
		Repayment of mortgage	
		Tax saving on BSI	1
		Tax relief on mortgage interest	1
		Utilisation of 24% tax band	
		Amount not utilised	1
		Tax saving/Advice	1
		Available	26
		Maximum	20

(b)	**(i)**	Tied advisers		1
		Independent advisers		1
			Maximum/Available	2
	(ii)	Carrying on of a business		1
		Authorisation		1
		Investments/Investment activities		1
			Maximum/Available	3
			Available	31
			Maximum	25

		Marks
5 (a) *Adjusted Schedule DI profit*		
Depreciation/Amortisation		1
Balancing allowance		1
Capital allowances		2
Lease deduction		2
Division of profits		1
Partners' 1996–97 Schedule DI assessments		
Alfred and Bertie		1
Claude		2
Daniel		2
	Maximum/Available	12
(b) (i) Schedule E 1990–91 to 1994–95		2
Schedule D 1994–95		1
Schedule D 1995–96		1
Schedule D 1996–97		1
	Maximum/Available	5
(ii) Limitation to 40%		1
Calculation of income taxable at 40%		1
Premium for 1996–97		1
Premium for 1995–96		1
Carry forward of unused relief		1
	Available	5
	Maximum	4
(c) *Sale of leasehold workshop*		
Overall calculation of capital gain		1
Lease percentage		1
Lease deductions (bonus)		1
Division of gain		1
Rollover relief		1
Purchase of freehold workshop		
Industrial buildings allowance		1
	Available	6
	Maximum	4
	Available	28
	Maximum	25

				Marks
6	(a)	(i)	Schedule A/Schedule A loss	1
			Capital gain/Capital loss	1
			Utilisation of loss of year ended 31.3.96	1
			Utilisation of loss of period ended 31.12.96	2
			Patent royalties/Deed of covenant	1
			Corporation tax	1
			ACT	2
			Maximum/Available	9
		(ii)	*Corporation tax refunds*	
			Year ended 30.9.93	1
			Period ended 31.3.94	1
			Year ended 31.3.95	1
			Relief under s.242	
			Availability of relief	1
			Tax refund	1
			Utilisation of losses	1
			Available	6
			Maximum	5
	(b)	(i)	*Surplus ACT*	
			Franked payments	1
			FII	1
			Calculation of surplus ACT (excluding maximum set-off)	1
			Maximum ACT set-off	
			Schedule DI profit/Debenture interest	1
			Loss relief/Schedule DIII	1
			Calculation of maximum ACT set-off (excluding claim under s.402)	1
			Claim under s.402	
			Corresponding period	1
			Calculation of claim	2
			Available	9
			Maximum	8
		(ii)	Carry back of ACT	1
			Carry forward of ACT	1
			51% subsidiary	1
			Utilisation/Maximum set-off	1
			Maximum	4
			Available	3
			Available	28
			Maximum	25